Dutch Oven

OBSESSION

Braised Pork Chops
with Vegetables and
Thyme (page 156)

ROBIN DONOVAN

Dutch Oven
OBSESSION

a cookbook for the only
pot in your life

SONOMA
PRESS

Front cover photography © StockFood/Jonathan Gregson; back cover photography © Stockfood/Ian Garlick; Stockfood/Miriam Garcia; Stockfood/Andrew Young

Interior photography © Stockfood/James Franco, p.2; Stocksy/Trent Lanz, p.8; Stockfood/Rua Castilho, p.20; Stockfood/Leigh Beisch, p.24; Stockfood/Gareth Morgans, p.31; Stockfood/PhotoCuisine/Tom Swalens, p.42; Stockfood/Aniko Takacs, p.47; Stockfood/Gräfe & Unzer Verlag/mona binner PHOTOGRAPHIE, p.56; Stockfood/Gräfe & Unzer Verlag /Klaus-Maria Einwanger, p.64; Stockfood/Maja Smend, p.69; Stockfood/Keller & Keller, p.76; Stockfood/Ian Garlick, p.86; Stockfood/PhotoCuisine/Pierre Louis Viel, p.93; Stockfood/ Gräfe & Unzer Verlag/Coco Lang, p.98; Stockfood/Jan-Peter Westermann, p.106; Stockfood/Martin Jacobs, p.113; Stockfood/Andrew Young, p.118; Stocksy/Trinette Reed, p.122; Stockfood/Julia Hoersch, p.139; Stockfood/Jim Norton, p.148; Stockfood/Martin Dyrlov, p.155; Stockfood/Tina Rupp, p.162; Stockfood/ Veslemøy Vråskar, p.176; Stockfood/Keller & Keller Photography, p.183; Stockfood/Miriam Garcia, p.192; Stockfood/PhotoCuisine/Studio, p.201; Stocksy/Javier Pardina, p.210.

Recipe featured in cover photo: Slow-Roasted Pork Roast with Onions and Carrots (Page 161)

ISBN: Print 978-1- 943451-50-0 | eBook 978-1- 943451-51-7

Contents

Introduction

When I picture my childhood kitchen, what I see is my mother, crisp apron tied around her waist, with a wooden spoon in one hand, an open copy of Julia Child's *Mastering the Art of French Cooking*—or another lauded cooking tome—on the counter, and a shiny enameled Dutch oven in Le Creuset's signature bright orange "flame" color bubbling away on the stove top. That Dutch oven came to represent for me the very foundation of what it means to be a great cook.

My mother was among that generation of American women who taught themselves to cook by watching Child on television or poring over her book. She started out by mastering French classics—things like bouillabaisse, ratatouille, and cassoulet filled her Dutch oven—but she quickly moved on to more adventurous fare. Smoky Brazilian black bean and pork *feijoada*, mysteriously chocolatey and spicy chicken mole, rich Greek moussaka, and spicy shrimp and sausage gumbo began to make appearances. On Thanksgiving her largest Dutch oven always held her classic savory bread stuffing. The next day the turkey carcass went in with water and veggies to make stock. Later, the leftover turkey meat became a Dutch oven turkey pot pie. For Hanukkah she made spiced brisket and, when we lucked out, jelly donuts for dessert. On Christmas morning, we had sweet, cinnamony French toast casserole straight from the pot.

By the time I left home, my devotion to the enameled Dutch oven was deeply ingrained, but I didn't get one of my own until many years later when I got married. It was the very first item I put on our wedding registry—a 5½-quart, kiwi-green, Le Creuset, round Dutch oven. My husband-to-be balked at both the size and the price. At the time, we lived in a tiny San Francisco apartment with a kitchen hardly larger than a closet. Most of our cookware, though completely functional, had been handed down by our mothers or picked up at tag sales and thrift stores. I admit that this stunning piece of high-end cookware seemed out of place in its first modest surroundings, but the minute I received that heavy box (thanks to friends who banded together to gift us with it), I was in love, and that love has endured over the years.

Though their popularity has ebbed and flowed, following the tide of cooking trends, enamel-coated cast iron Dutch ovens have been a staple of well-equipped kitchens since the 1920s. Even when every restaurant in town is flaunting grilled meats, quick and light sautés, or even raw foods, at home, a satisfying soup, tender roast, hearty stew, or decadent cheese-and-pasta dish with a crispy bread-crumb topping always seems to be in style.

Since my wedding, I've used my big green Dutch oven to cook thousands of dishes, from applesauce to zarzuela. It makes regular appearances on my stove top to cook everything from my son's favorite Matzo Ball Soup (page 70) to my husband's beloved Mexican Pork and Sweet Potato Stew (page 82) to my own favorite, White Bean Stew with Spanish Chorizo (page 154). In the summer my family loves to visit pick-it-yourself fruit orchards where we load up on vine- or tree-ripened berries, peaches, nectarines, apricots, cherries, and plums. My big green Dutch oven is the perfect vessel for cooking down the fruit and turning it into sweet, spreadable jams and jellies.

And I can't neglect to mention that a Dutch oven makes the most delectable upside-down cake, such as the Caramelized Pear Upside-Down Cake (page 194). No matter what fruit you choose, whether it be pineapples, peaches, bananas, pears, or some creative combination, the sugars caramelize to perfection, and the cake develops just the right amount of toothsome crunch on the outside while remaining pillowy and soft on the inside.

I like to think of this book as a love letter to my Dutch oven. With more than 100 recipes, the book will show you just how versatile— and downright obsession-worthy—an enameled Dutch oven is. It is ideal for making quick one-pot meals for a family; cooking tough meats and hearty vegetables to tender perfection; braising and roasting everything from cauliflower to lamb shanks; simmering soups, broths, and sauces for hours; making irresistible desserts; and even baking bread. Whatever the occasion, the Dutch oven has you covered. It could very well prove to be truly the only pot you need.

Chapter One

Going Dutch

With an enameled Dutch oven, the possibilities are endless. You can create enticing meals perfect for every day of the week, not to mention simple breads, desserts, and more. Synonymous with slow cooking, the Dutch oven also comes in handy on a busy weeknight, often limiting your meal cleanup to just one pot. Perfect for hearty dinners, it also works wonders when cooking for date night, or whipping up crowd-pleasing party treats. It's equally great for deep-frying food without making a mess and baking perfectly golden-brown bread from scratch. As it's the most versatile pot in your kitchen, it's easy to become obsessed with your Dutch oven. In this chapter, we'll take some time to remember why.

THE OBSESSION

There are countless reasons why enameled cast iron Dutch ovens have a hold on the hearts of so many cooks. Simply put, a Dutch oven is a majestic pot with a storied heritage, and it can do just about anything when it comes to cooking delicious food.

Rich with History

Cast iron cookware has been around for more than 2,000 years, dating back to the Chinese Han Dynasty (206 BCE to 220 CE), but by the early part of the 18th century, the Dutch were at the forefront of its production. They used molds made of dry sand, rather than the loam or clay soil used elsewhere in Europe, to cast their iron pots, giving them a smooth surface. According to John G. Ragsdale in his book *Dutch Ovens Chronicled*, an Englishman named Abraham Darcy went to the Netherlands in 1704 to study the makers' superior casting process. Four years later, Darcy patented a similar casting process using dry sand molds. Ragsdale theorizes that this is how the pots came to be known as "Dutch ovens." They were soon distributed widely throughout Britain and shipped to its colonies in the Americas.

Still, cast iron cookware remained uncoated, which meant that it had to be seasoned and cared for in its particular way. Users had other issues as well. Cast iron cookware wasn't ideal for cooking foods with high acidity, as excessive amounts of iron could leach from the pan into the food. Also, some people simply didn't care for the rustic look of bare cast iron.

In their first attempts to address these issues, manufacturers offered versions of cast iron cookware that were plated with nickel or chrome on the outside, giving them a more appealing look. These plated versions were considerably more expensive, and since the interior of the pan was left uncoated, the other issues persisted. So, in the 1920s, French manufacturers, including Le Creuset, began using a vitreous enamel to coat the pots, both inside and out. The process involves grinding glass, color pigments, and minerals into a fine powder; spraying the powder onto the cast pots; and then firing them to melt the glass and fuse the mixture with the iron. The resulting enamel coating makes the pots at once more attractive, easier to care for, and in many ways more functional. The coated pots don't need to be seasoned, are easier to clean, and won't react with acidic foods.

The enameling process added considerably to the cost, however, and the cookware was thus elevated from cookware for the masses to luxury status. In an effort to distinguish their high-end enameled products from the less expensive uncoated versions, French manufacturers dubbed theirs "French ovens," but the name never really took. Technically, a Dutch oven is an uncoated cast iron pot, while an enamel-coated one is a French oven, but in reality, people use the terms interchangeably. Most people use the name "Dutch oven" to refer to both the coated and uncoated cast iron pots.

Versatility

Because they can be used over high or low heat, on the stove top or in the oven, Dutch ovens are impressively versatile. They are the perfect vessel for making long-simmering sauces, soups, or broths on the stove top; hearty oven-braised roasts and stews; and even dishes that require both stove top and oven cooking, like a decadent macaroni-and-cheese casserole topped with a layer of crispy bread crumbs.

Durability

Enameled Dutch ovens are among the most durable cookware there is. They eliminate the problems of rusting, leaching iron, and interactions with acidic foods that beleaguer bare cast iron pots. These enameled pots can be scrubbed by hand using dish soap or even run through the dishwasher. And, of course, laborious seasoning is unnecessary.

Superior Cooking Qualities

Because cast iron pots are thicker and heavier than those made of steel, copper, or aluminum, they conduct heat better, faster, and more uniformly, and they retain heat better than their lighter-weight counterparts. Even when you add cold food to a hot cast iron Dutch oven, the temperature remains nearly constant.

The Dutch oven's large volume allows it to hold larger quantities of food than skillets and other vessels can. And its high walls also make it great for things like deep-frying because the walls contain splatters and reduce kitchen mess.

The Original Slow Cooker

Dutch ovens are the original slow cookers. While they don't have quite the same "set it and forget it" convenience as an electric slow cooker, they still work in much the same manner. Because the bottom, sides, and lid all conduct and radiate heat the same way, the pot acts just like an oven by providing a total surround, self-contained cooking area. The heavy lid traps in moisture to prevent foods from drying out as they cook and also supports sustained low-heat cooking. As a result, tough meats, fibrous vegetables, and other sturdier foods are cooked to tender perfection as they are infused with deep flavor over a long, slow cooking period.

Electric slow cookers are known for keeping food at a very low (around 212°F) temperature, because this allows them to cook food very slowly, but the drawback is that they can't achieve higher temperatures. The advantage of sustained very low heat cooking is that you can put the ingredients into the pot in the morning, turn it on, head to work for the day, and return home to a perfectly cooked meal 8 or 10 hours later. But this very low temperature doesn't encourage the caramelization or browning that gives food the deep, complex flavors we love. A Dutch oven can also be heated to high temperatures and used to brown or caramelize ingredients, giving food that sweet or crispy goodness something electric slow cookers cannot do—and then set at lower temperatures on the stove top or in the oven, offering cooks the best of both worlds.

THE MOVES

As you get to know your Dutch oven, you'll be delighted by its many talents. It will quickly become your everyday, go-to pot for just about every type of cooking you can think of.

Braising. The thick walls and heavy lid maintain steady heat and trap in moisture, creating an ideal environment for long, slow braising either on the stove top or in the oven.

Roasting. Using your Dutch oven to roast meats offers numerous advantages. For one, you can brown the meat on the stove top and then put it straight into the oven without having to dirty a second pan. The high walls of the Dutch oven also contain splatters, creating less mess in your oven. And, most importantly, the sustained, even heat of the Dutch oven provides a great environment to cook meat without drying it out.

Baking. Because of its superior heat retention and conduction, a Dutch oven can help your regular home oven perform like a professional baking oven, providing intense full-surround heat. Baking bread in a covered Dutch oven traps in moisture, giving the bread the crisp, crackly crust bakeries use high-end humidifiers to achieve. Sugary desserts achieve unbelievable caramelization.

Dutch Oven Cooking Tips

There is nothing particularly difficult about Dutch oven cooking, but knowing a bit about the Dutch oven's unique traits, likes, and dislikes will help you enjoy yours to its fullest.

> **Because of its ability to retain heat efficiently, use low heat settings for both stovetop and oven cooking**. Low to medium heat is usually sufficient. For best results, allow your pot to heat gradually and thoroughly. Once hot, low heat settings are usually sufficient.

> **High heat should only be used for boiling water or for reducing sauces or stocks**. An overheated pan can cause food to stick and burn.

> **For maximum efficiency, match the pan size to the burner size for stovetop cooking**. A small pot on a large burner can overheat and become damaged or cause food to stick. The flames of a gas burner should never extend outside of the pot's base.

> **Always cover the bottom of the pot with liquid or fat before heating, and never let the pot boil dry**. Dry cooking can damage the enamel.

> **Use silicone, wooden, or heat-resistant plastic spoons, spatulas, and other utensils to protect the enamel coating**. Metal tools, such as spoons or whisks, can be used so long as they are used gently and not scraped across the enamel surface or knocked against the rim of the pot.

> **While the cast iron pot itself is ovenproof at any temperature, some Dutch ovens have handles that are safe only at low temperatures**. Check the manufacturer's recommendations regarding heat limits. Cast iron and stainless steel handles and knobs are safe to use at any oven temperature, while plastic or wood may be safe to use only at low temperatures. If you have non-ovenproof handles or knobs, they are usually easily replaced with ovenproof ones.

Frying. While most people associate the Dutch oven more with braising, simmering, and roasting, it also makes a great stovetop deep-fryer. Because of its high heat retention and great heat conduction, it's possible to get oil to the screaming hot temperature needed for a good, crispy deep-fried coating. The Dutch oven's high walls keep that oil from splattering all over your kitchen, whether you're deep-frying apple fritters, crisping bacon, or stir-frying vegetables.

Simmering. Start by caramelizing your onions and garlic, sautéing your aromatics, and deglazing the pot over high heat. Whether you add bones and water, beans and broth, or meat and vegetables, the Dutch oven will bring it to a simmer in no time. Keep the heat low for a long, slow simmer. Cover the pot to retain liquid; uncover it to reduce or thicken your dish.

THE ONE FOR YOU

Chances are you already have a Dutch oven. But no Dutch oven cookbook would be complete without a quick look at what's available. Plus you might be interested in expanding your collection to include mini cocottes or even upgrading.

My Favorites

Lodge, the esteemed maker of bare cast iron skillets and Dutch ovens, now makes a line of enameled cast iron cookware that gets high marks for its functionality and aesthetically pleasing design. Its 5½-quart round enameled Dutch oven has large handles that make it easy to maneuver, ovenproof stainless steel knobs, and a surface area wide enough for good searing and to allow ample evaporation for braised dishes and reductions. Retailing for around $80, it offers great value, though it has garnered complaints about the enamel chipping.

Martha Stewart makes a sleek 6-quart round enameled cast iron Dutch oven with classic straight-sided styling and an ovenproof stainless steel lid handle. Its quality rivals that of more expensive brands, yet it sells for under $100. The only downside for me is the celebrity branding that's cast right into the lid, but if you don't mind that (or are a big Martha fan) and are looking for a good, solid Dutch oven at an affordable price, you won't be disappointed.

Le Creuset and **Staub** are the gold standards of enameled Dutch ovens. With their ample size, heavy-duty cast iron, and virtually chip-proof enamel coatings, the Dutch ovens from both of these brands are high-quality pieces of equipment that will last for generations. The downside is that you'll pay a pretty penny—both brands' 5½-quart Dutch ovens carry price tags of around $300. They're worth it if you plan to use the pot often and want to hold onto it for the next several decades or pass it on to someone you love. (They also make fantastic wedding gifts. I'm just saying.)

Does Size Matter?

Dutch ovens come in a wide range of sizes. Mini cocottes come in sizes ranging from 4 to 12 ounces, and you'll find larger Dutch ovens that run the gamut from 1 to 14 quarts. If you are looking to buy your first Dutch oven, I recommend a medium-size one. The major brands all make one in the 5- to 6-quart range, which is perfect for recipes yielding 4 to 6 servings, making it a good size for the average family meal, plus leftovers if you're lucky. This size easily fits a whole chicken or duck, pork loin, chuck roast, lamb shank, handful of short ribs, or few pounds of pork shoulder. It is also the perfect size for making pots of soup and chili, pot pies, lasagna, enchiladas, or cakes and fruit crisps.

What is a cocotte?

Cocotte is simply the French word for a Dutch oven. As mentioned earlier, when French manufacturers began coating Dutch ovens with enamel, they wanted to distinguish their high-end products from the less-expensive uncoated cast iron versions, so they called them "French ovens," or "cocottes," instead. The name didn't really catch on, although you'll still hear the term *French oven* now and then to refer to the enamel-coated cast iron Dutch oven. Today the word *cocotte* is most often used to refer to the miniature version of the Dutch oven (mini cocottes), while the term *Dutch oven* is used to refer to both the coated and uncoated versions of the larger lidded cast iron pot.

Oval Dutch ovens are fine for many applications, but they take up an inordinate amount of space on your stove and are awkward for things like quiches or cakes that you want to be able to cut into nice wedges for serving. As a result, if you are only going to have one Dutch oven or if you are looking for a mainstay, do-it-all pot for your kitchen, I highly recommend sticking with a round one.

With the exception of a few appetizer and dessert recipes cooked in mini cocottes, the recipes in this book were all tested using a 5½-quart Dutch oven. If you happen to have a slightly larger or slightly smaller version, don't fret. Your recipes will still turn out just fine. If you wish to use one that is significantly smaller or larger, you'll want to adjust the recipes to fit.

Mini Cocottes

Mini cocottes are adorable miniature versions of Dutch ovens. They come in sizes ranging from 4 to 12 ounces. Mini cocottes are most often used for cooking individual servings of foods such as appetizers, casseroles, pot pies, or cakes, custards, and other desserts. Mini Herb and Gruyère Soufflés in Mini Cocottes (page 50) and Butterscotch Custard in Mini Cocottes (page 207) are just a couple of my favorite recipes using mini cocottes that are featured in this book. If you are thinking about expanding your Dutch oven collection, they are a great addition because they open up entirely new possibilities.

THE LOVE

While I have a passion for cast iron cookware of every type, I do have a special love for my enameled cast iron Dutch ovens, simply because they are so easy to care for. Here are my tips for treating your Dutch oven the way it deserves to be treated:

> Let the pot cool before washing. Never plunge a hot pot into cold water, as this can cause the enamel to crack or chip.

> Wash your Dutch oven either by hand or in the dishwasher using normal dish soap or dishwasher detergent. Note that repeated washing in the dishwasher may dull the finish, but this will not impact performance.

> If you have stuck-on food, let the pot soak with warm water in it for 15 minutes or so before scrubbing.

Eight Surprising Ways to Use Your Dutch Oven

With their even heat distribution, Dutch ovens are ideal for roasting and braising, but that's not all they can do. Not by a long shot. Here are some of my favorite surprises:

1 **Home-Baked Bread.** If you dream of making artisan-style bread at home, the Dutch oven makes it possible. Its heavy lid traps the bread's moisture in the pot, resulting in bakery-worthy bread with a crispy, crackly crust and moist, chewy interior.

2 **Fried Chicken.** A Dutch oven is great for deep-frying. The oil achieves and maintains a high temperature that produces crunchy, golden-brown chicken that's never greasy.

3 **Pot Pies.** Cook the filling in the pot, top it with a pastry crust, and pop it in the oven until the filling is bubbling and the crust is flaky and golden brown.

4 **Messy One-Pot Lasagna.** Cook the sauce in the pot, stir in broken lasagna noodles, dollop ricotta cheese over the top, and sprinkle with shredded mozzarella and Parmesan cheese. Bake until bubbling and golden brown.

5 **Donuts and Fritters.** See fried chicken above. For all the same reasons, a Dutch oven is the best way to make crispy fried donuts, fritters, and other deep-fried, sweet treats.

6 **Fruit Crisps.** The Dutch oven's high, even heat caramelizes sweet fruits like no other pan, and your topping develops a

delectable golden-brown crunch. Plus, the high sides prevent excessive oven splattering.

7 **Upside-Down Cakes.** As with fruit crisps, the high, even heat of the cast iron does an amazing job of caramelizing the fruit, creating a stunning and deeply delicious top (bottom) that is irresistible.

8 **Sweet and Savory Fruit Jams.** The wide cooking area of a Dutch oven is perfect for reducing the liquid, the even and sustained heat of a heavy cast iron pot is ideal for achieving the high temperature required to achieve a set point, and the enamel coating makes the pot nonreactive and fairly nonstick.

Camp Cooking

Google the phrase "Dutch oven cooking," and the first results that will come up won't be of shiny, brightly colored enameled pots filled with beef bourguignon. Instead you'll find a slew of images of, and recipes for, the uncoated cast iron Dutch ovens intended for cooking over hot coals in an outdoor fire pit or campfire. For camp or outdoor Dutch oven cooking, the uncoated cast iron Dutch ovens are put directly over hot coals in an outdoor fire pit or campfire, usually with additional hot coals placed on top. It's a completely different world, but if you're as enthusiastic about outdoor cooking as you are about indoor cooking, it's one that is worth exploring. Outdoor-style Dutch ovens usually have a flat, rimmed lid that is designed to hold the coals. Many also have three legs on the bottom to make them more stable when you put them in a fire pit over the hot coals.

Over a campfire, Dutch ovens are usually used to cook homey fare—think franks 'n' beans, ground beef chili, cheesy casseroles, and tamale pie—but many of the recipes in this book could easily be adapted for camp cooking.

CAST IRON DUTCH OVEN CARE

Uncoated cast iron requires special attention. First, it should be seasoned (coated with oil and left in a hot oven for an hour or two) before use. Second, it's best to use only hot water for washing (no dish soap). If the cast iron has been well seasoned, food particles should come right off with just a bit of elbow grease, some hot water, and a sponge or a stiff, natural- or plastic-bristle (not wire) brush. Boiling water, kosher salt, or baking soda can all be called on to deal with stubborn stuck-on food. And last, but definitely not least, an uncoated cast iron pot should always be thoroughly dried immediately after washing to prevent rust. Ideally, you'll also rub it each time with a bit of vegetable oil to maintain its seasoning.

> If necessary, use a nylon or soft plastic scrubber or brush to scrub off stuck-on food.

> Do not use harsh abrasives or metallic cleaning pads.

> If your pot develops stubborn stains, either inside or outside, make a paste by mixing a few spoonfuls of baking soda with a bit of water. Spread the mixture over the stained surface, and let it sit overnight. In the morning, scrub with a nylon or soft plastic scrubber until you achieve the desired results. You may have to repeat this process a few times.

> Always dry your pot thoroughly before storing.

> If you store your enameled cast iron pans stacked, or stack other pans inside of them, protect them with a sheet of cardboard in between to prevent scratching or chipping of the enamel coating.

THE RECIPES

The more than 100 recipes in this book showcase foods and cooking methods that are a perfect match for your Dutch oven. From weekday breakfasts to fancy brunch dishes, casual lunches to dinner parties, recipes can be found here for every occasion, proving that there is little your Dutch oven can't do.

The recipes are straightforward, creative, and perfect for any day of the week. Many of the recipes are quick and easy, with start-to-finish times of less than 60 minutes and a good number of main dishes taking 45 minutes or less to prepare (the latter are labeled "Weeknight Win"). Recipes for more leisurely weekend meals are also included, for when you have a little more time to spend in the kitchen and want to prepare something special. There are even a few exceptional appetizer and dessert recipes for when you really want to wow your dinner guests.

Whether you are looking for simple one-pot meals to get weeknight dinners on the table fast or hoping to find unexpected uses for your favorite kitchen pot, this book has something for you.

Oven-Baked Tomato, Olive, and Feta Frittata (page 41)

Chapter Two

Breakfast & Brunch

Apple-Cinnamon French Toast Casserole

SERVES 8 • PREP: 15 MINUTES • COOK: 40 MINUTES

ONE POT

Butter or oil for preparing
the Dutch oven

8 eggs, at room temperature

3 cups milk

⅓ cup brown sugar

1 tablespoon vanilla extract

1 loaf (about 16 ounces)
bread, cut into cubes

5 apples, peeled and
cut into cubes

⅓ cup sugar

1 tablespoon lemon juice

1 teaspoon cinnamon

Pinch of salt

2 tablespoons melted butter

This comforting combination of bread, milk, eggs, sugar, and fruit makes for a fun and filling morning meal. It's festive enough for brunch on a holiday or other special occasion, but much simpler to make than French toast, which is cooked to order. In fact, you can prepare the dish the day before and refrigerate it overnight. Just add 20 to 30 minutes onto the baking time, since it will be cold when it goes into the oven.

1 Preheat the oven to 375°F and coat the bottom and sides of the Dutch oven with butter or oil.

2 In the Dutch oven, beat together the eggs, milk, brown sugar, and vanilla. Stir in the bread cubes.

3 In a large bowl, combine the apples, sugar, lemon juice, cinnamon, salt, and melted butter and stir to mix well.

4 Evenly spread the apple mixture over the bread mixture. Bake, uncovered, for 40 minutes.

Seasonal Swap: In the fall and winter, either apples or pears work wonderfully in this breakfast casserole, but in the summer, try substituting fresh, ripe peaches.

Banana-Nut Breakfast Bread Pudding with a Kick

SERVES 6 ⁘ PREP: 10 MINUTES, PLUS 30 MINUTES TO SOAK BREAD ⁘ COOK: 40 MINUTES

4 large eggs

1½ cups whole milk

1 teaspoon vanilla extract

8 thick slices bread,
    cut into cubes

3 medium bananas,
    peeled and diced

½ cup pecans

½ cup (packed) brown sugar

2 tablespoons dark rum

4 tablespoons unsalted
    butter, cut into
    small pieces

It's like having bananas Foster for breakfast! This slightly decadent version of French toast is easy to prep ahead and pop in the oven for a special breakfast or brunch (think Christmas morning). If you're not the booze-in-the-morning type, feel free to leave out the rum.

1 In the Dutch oven, whisk together the eggs, milk, and vanilla. Add the bread cubes and stir to coat well. Let soak for at least 30 minutes.

2 Preheat the oven to 400°F.

3 In a medium bowl, stir together the bananas, pecans, brown sugar, and rum. Spread over the top of the bread mixture in the Dutch oven. Dot with the butter. Cover and bake for 35 to 40 minutes, until the pudding is cooked through, puffed, and golden on top.

4 Serve warm.

Seasonal Swap: For a summery take on this dish, you can substitute peaches or nectarines for the bananas. In the fall, you could use pears or apples.

Blueberries and Cream Cheese Coffee Cake

SERVES 8 · PREP: 10 MINUTES · COOK: 55 MINUTES

FOR THE CAKE

¾ cup unsalted butter,
    at room temperature,
    plus additional for pre-
    paring the Dutch oven

2 ¼ cups all-purpose flour

¾ cup sugar

½ teaspoon fine sea salt

1 large egg

¾ cup buttermilk

½ teaspoon baking soda

½ teaspoon baking powder

1 teaspoon vanilla extract

FOR THE FROSTING

8 ounces cream cheese,
    at room temperature

⅓ cup sugar

1 large egg

1 teaspoon vanilla extract

FOR ASSEMBLING THE CAKE

1 ¼ cups fresh blueberries,
    divided

½ cup sliced almonds

¾ cup powdered sugar,
    for a garnish

This moist buttermilk cake is topped with a sweet layer of creamy topping, plump blueberries, and crunchy, toasted almonds. This gorgeous breakfast cake is a perfect accompaniment to a hot cup of coffee. You'll want to make this once a week during blueberry season.

TO MAKE THE CAKE

1 Preheat the oven to 350°F. Coat the inside of the Dutch oven with butter.

2 In a large bowl, mix together the flour, butter, sugar, and salt until the mixture is crumbly. Remove 1 cup of the mixture and reserve for later.

3 Add the egg, buttermilk, baking soda, baking powder, and vanilla to the remaining mixture in the bowl. Stir to mix, then transfer the mixture to the prepared pot, smoothing it out into an even layer.

TO MAKE THE FROSTING

In a small bowl, using an electric mixer, cream together the cream cheese and sugar until smooth. Beat in the egg and vanilla. >>

TO ASSEMBLE THE CAKE

1 Pour the mixture over the top of the cake, spreading it out in an even layer and leaving a 1½-inch rim around the edge of the cake.

2 Scatter 1 cup of the blueberries over the cream cheese mixture.

3 In a small bowl stir together the reserved flour mixture and the almonds. Sprinkle this mixture over the top of the cake.

4 Bake, uncovered, in the preheated oven for 50 to 55 minutes, or until the center is set.

5 Remove from the oven and let cool completely. Sprinkle the powdered sugar over the top and serve, garnished with the remaining ¼ cup of blueberries.

Seasonal Swap: You can substitute any berries—strawberries, blackberries, boysenberries—for the blueberries if they are out of season. Or try pitted cherries or sliced peaches or nectarines.

Pecan-Caramel Coffee Cake

SERVES 8 • PREP: 10 MINUTES • COOK: 30 MINUTES

Butter or oil for preparing the Dutch oven

FOR THE FILLING

2 tablespoons unsalted butter, softened

¾ cup (packed) brown sugar

1 large egg, lightly beaten

⅓ cup milk

⅓ cup chopped pecans

FOR THE CAKE BATTER

2 cups all-purpose flour

¾ cup sugar

1 tablespoon instant coffee

2½ teaspoons baking powder

1 teaspoon fine sea salt

2 large eggs

⅔ cup milk

½ cup vegetable oil

With a sweet, crunchy caramel and pecan filling swirled throughout the batter, this coffee cake is a sweet treat that will start any day right. A hot cup of coffee or tea is all you need to accompany it, but a bowl of fresh peaches or berries would be lovely alongside.

Preheat the oven to 375°F and coat the inside of the Dutch oven with butter or oil.

TO MAKE THE FILLING

In a medium saucepan, combine the butter, brown sugar, and egg and stir to mix well. Stir in the milk and cook, stirring, over medium heat, until the mixture thickens and becomes smooth, about 3 minutes. Stir in the pecans.

TO MAKE THE CAKE BATTER

1 In a large bowl, whisk together the flour, sugar, coffee, baking powder, and salt.

2 In a separate large bowl, beat together the eggs, milk, and oil. Add the flour mixture to the egg mixture and mix just until combined.

3 Transfer the batter to the prepared Dutch oven and spread the filling mixture over the top. Use a knife to swirl the filling into the batter.

4 Cover and bake for 25 to 30 minutes, until a tester inserted into the center comes out clean.

Cinnamon-Glazed Apple Fritters

MAKES 12 FRITTERS • PREP: 15 MINUTES • COOK: 15 MINUTES

2 quarts peanut or
vegetable oil, for frying

FOR THE GLAZE

2 cups powdered sugar

1 teaspoon vanilla extract

1 teaspoon cinnamon

2 tablespoons milk, plus
additional if needed

FOR THE BATTER

1 cup flour

1½ teaspoons
baking powder

½ teaspoon salt

2 tablespoons sugar

½ to 1 teaspoon cinnamon
(depending on how
much you want)

1 large egg, beaten

½ cup plus
1 tablespoon milk

1½ cups (about 3 whole)
peeled and diced apples

Deep-frying is one of the most overlooked ways to use a Dutch oven to its best advantage, and these sweet fritters are a great way to test out this cooking method. Thanks to the superior heat conduction and retention of cast iron, the oil gets really hot and stays that way (even when you add cold food). The high sides of the Dutch oven keep the oil from splattering. The end result is a fritter that is crisp on the outside and pillowy cinnamon-apple goodness on the inside.

Fill the Dutch oven about half full with oil and heat over medium-high heat until the oil registers 375°F on a deep-fry thermometer. Line a plate with paper towels.

TO MAKE THE GLAZE

While the oil is heating, make the glaze. In a medium bowl, stir together the powdered sugar, vanilla, cinnamon, and milk. If the glaze is too thick, add more milk, 1 teaspoon at a time, until the desired consistency is reached.

TO MAKE THE BATTER

In a large bowl, whisk together the flour, baking powder, salt, sugar, and cinnamon. Stir in the egg and milk until incorporated. Stir in the apples and mix well.

TO ASSEMBLE THE FRITTERS

1 Once the oil is hot, drop the batter by the heaping tablespoonful into hot oil, cooking three or four fritters at a time, being careful not to crowd the pan. Cook until the fritters are deep golden brown, about 2 minutes per side. Using tongs, a slotted spoon, or a spider, transfer the cooked fritters to the prepared plate.

2 Once all the fritters have been fried, drop each one separately into the glaze mixture, turn it over to coat the whole thing, and then transfer it to a wire rack set over a baking sheet or a piece of parchment. Let cool completely. Serve at room temperature.

Essential Technique: Getting the oil hot enough is crucial for making crisp, golden-brown, not-greasy fritters. Invest in a simple, inexpensive deep-fry thermometer to make sure your oil reaches 375°F and stays near there the whole time you are frying.

Portobello Mushroom Egg Bake

SERVES 4 • PREP: 10 MINUTES • COOK: 30 MINUTES

ONE POT

4 good-size Portobello mushroom caps, stemmed

2 to 3 large Yukon gold potatoes, cut into thin wedges

1 pint cherry tomatoes

2 tablespoons olive oil

2 garlic cloves, minced

Kosher salt

Freshly ground black pepper

4 large eggs

2 tablespoons chopped flat-leaf parsley

Meaty mushrooms make a perfect and delightful baking vessel for eggs. Roast them along with potatoes and tomatoes, and you have a flavorful one-pot breakfast or brunch dish. For extra flavor and a bit of decadence, top the dish with crumbled goat or feta cheese, if you like.

1 Preheat the oven to 425°F.

2 In the Dutch oven, toss the mushroom caps, potatoes, and tomatoes with the olive oil and garlic. Season with salt and pepper. Spread the mixture out into an even layer in the pot, and roast in the preheated oven for about 15 minutes.

3 Remove the pot from the oven and stir the vegetables. Arrange the mushroom caps so that they are gill-side up. Crack an egg into each cap, season with a little salt and pepper, and return the pot to the oven to bake for another 10 to 12 minutes, until the whites of the eggs are opaque and the yolk is still a bit runny.

4 Serve immediately, garnished with parsley.

Dutch Oven Eggs Benedict with Hollandaise

SERVES 6 • PREP: 15 MINUTES • COOK: 55 MINUTES

FOR THE CASSEROLE

6 English muffins, split and cut into 1-inch cubes

2 tablespoons unsalted butter

12 ounces diced Canadian bacon

10 large eggs, divided

2 cups milk

½ cup heavy cream

1½ teaspoons Dijon mustard

½ teaspoon kosher salt

½ teaspoon freshly ground black pepper

Nothing says brunch like eggs Benedict, but toasting all those muffins, poaching all those eggs, and whisking and simmering the sauce can be tedious, and doing all that makes it difficult to serve all of your guests at once. This casserole is the perfect solution—it's got all the flavors of the classic dish but is baked all at once in the Dutch oven while you whip up a quick hollandaise sauce in the blender.

TO MAKE THE CASSEROLE

1 Preheat the oven to 400°F.

2 Place the English muffin cubes on a baking sheet and toast in the oven for about 10 minutes, until lightly browned.

3 Meanwhile, melt the butter in the Dutch oven over medium-high heat. Add the Canadian bacon and cook, stirring, until it begins to brown, about 4 minutes. Remove from the heat.

4 When the bread is toasted, reduce the oven temperature to 350°F. Add the toasted bread cubes to the Dutch oven and stir to mix with the Canadian bacon. Spread the mixture out into an even layer.

5 In a large bowl, whisk together the eggs, milk, cream, mustard, salt, and pepper. Pour the mixture over the bread cubes in the Dutch oven and bake, uncovered, for 40 to 45 minutes, until the casserole is puffed, just set in the center, and golden brown on top.

2 large egg yolks

2 tablespoons freshly
squeezed lemon juice,
plus additional if needed

1¼ cups (2½ sticks)
unsalted butter, melted
until foamy

Kosher salt

Freshly ground
black pepper

Pinch of cayenne pepper

¼ cup minced fresh chives,
for garnish

TO MAKE THE HOLLANDAISE SAUCE

1 While the casserole is in the oven, place the egg yolks and lemon juice in a blender, cover, and blend until well combined.

2 With the blender running, pour the melted butter into the blender in a slow, thin stream (discard the milk solids left in the bottom of the melted butter dish or pan). Blend until the sauce becomes thick and creamy. Season with salt, pepper, and cayenne. Add additional lemon juice if desired.

3 To serve, cut the casserole into wedges and serve warm, drizzled with the hollandaise sauce and garnished with chives.

Essential Technique: If you are concerned about using raw egg yolks, you can make a more traditional hollandaise sauce that gently heats the yolks. In the top of a double boiler set over simmering water, whisk the yolks until they become thick and creamy (use an instant-read thermometer to make sure you don't overcook the yolks; the temperature shouldn't exceed 150°F). Remove the pot from the heat and slowly drizzle in the melted butter while whisking continuously. Once it is emulsified, add the lemon juice, salt, pepper, and cayenne.

Goat Cheese, Scallion & Fresh Herb Quiche with a Sweet Potato Crust

SERVES 8 • PREP: 10 MINUTES • COOK: 45 MINUTES

Butter for preparing
the Dutch oven

2 medium sweet potatoes,
peeled and sliced into
very thin rounds, about
1/16 inch thick

6 large eggs

1/2 cup whole milk

1/4 teaspoon kosher salt

1/4 teaspoon freshly ground
black pepper

4 scallions, thinly sliced

2 tablespoons chopped
fresh oregano

4 ounces crumbled
goat cheese

Sweet potatoes are truly a wonder—so delicious and so good for you at the same time. Here they make a fabulous crust for a luscious and creamy filling of eggs, cheese, and fresh herbs. Serve this beautiful quiche for a special brunch, or make one on Sunday and warm up slices each day throughout the week for a quick, healthy, and satisfying breakfast. Using a mandolin to slice the sweet potato will help you get it into very thin, even rounds.

1 Preheat the oven to 350°F and coat the inside of the Dutch oven with butter.

2 Create a crust with the sweet potato slices by arranging them, slightly overlapping one another, to cover the bottom of the Dutch oven. Trim some of the slices so that you can stand them on their flat edges to form a wall around the sides of the Dutch oven. You will end up with a bottom and sides that are several layers deep with sweet potato slices. Bake the crust for 20 minutes.

3 Meanwhile, in a large bowl, whisk together the eggs, milk, salt, and pepper until combined. Stir in the scallions, oregano, and goat cheese.

4 Remove the crust from the oven and increase the oven temperature to 400°F.

5 Pour the egg mixture into the crust and bake for about 25 minutes, until eggs are set in the middle. Let cool for a few minutes before slicing into wedges. Serve warm.

Smoked Salmon and Cream Cheese Quiche

SERVES 6 TO 8 · PREP: 20 MINUTES, PLUS 15 MINUTES TO COOL · COOK: 40 MINUTES

4 medium russet potatoes (about 2 pounds), peeled and grated on the large holes of a box grater or using the grating attachment in a food processor

1 teaspoon kosher salt, divided

¾ teaspoon freshly ground black pepper, divided

2 tablespoons unsalted butter

2 tablespoons vegetable oil

6 large eggs, at room temperature

4 ounces cream cheese, at room temperature

1¼ cups half-and-half

6 ounces smoked salmon, chopped

2 tablespoons chopped fresh dill

Make It a Meal: Serve wedges of this quiche with fresh fruit salad and glasses of freshly squeezed orange juice or mimosas for a special brunch.

This clever quiche construction combines all the goodness of two favorite meals—bagels and lox and potato pancakes—into one savory pie. A crispy shredded-potato crust is filled with a mixture of eggs, cream cheese, and half-and-half, studded with bits of flavorful smoked salmon, and laced with fresh dill.

1 Preheat the oven to 350°F.

2 In a large bowl, toss together the shredded potatoes, ½ teaspoon of salt, and ½ teaspoon of pepper. Transfer the potatoes to a dish towel, and wring out any excess liquid.

3 In the Dutch oven, heat the butter with the oil over medium-high heat. Add the shredded potatoes, pressing them into the bottom and sides of the pot to form a crust. Continue to cook, pressing the crust into the pot, until the potatoes begin to brown, about 10 minutes. Remove from the heat.

4 In a large bowl, whisk together the eggs and cream cheese until combined. Add the half-and-half, salmon, dill, the remaining ½ teaspoon of salt and ¼ teaspoon of pepper.

5 Pour the egg mixture into the potato crust and bake for about 30 minutes, until the egg mixture is set and golden brown on top. Let cool for about 15 minutes before serving. Serve warm.

Bacon and Apple Frittata with Cheddar Cheese

SERVES 6 TO 8 · PREP: 15 MINUTES · COOK: 25 MINUTES

6 slices bacon

12 large eggs

1½ cups shredded sharp Cheddar cheese, divided

½ teaspoon kosher salt

¼ teaspoon freshly ground black pepper

2 tablespoons unsalted butter

3 tart, crisp apples, like Granny Smith or Fuji, peeled, cored, and thinly sliced

Essential Technique: The Dutch oven is very heavy and will be hot when you go to invert the frittata onto the cutting board. Use two thick oven mitts to hold the pot's handles and the cutting board as you invert it. You can also serve the frittata directly from the Dutch oven if you prefer.

I love making frittatas for all sorts of occasions, since they can include a wide range of flavors and ingredients, can easily be made ahead, and are delicious warm, cold, or at room temperature. This frittata is unusual in that it combines tart apples with smoky bacon and sharp cheddar cheese.

1 Preheat the oven to 450°F.

2 In the Dutch oven, cook the bacon over medium-high heat until crispy, about 5 minutes. Drain the slices on paper towels and then crumble.

3 In a large bowl, whisk the eggs, then whisk in 1 cup of Cheddar cheese, the salt, and the pepper.

4 Drain the bacon fat from the Dutch oven, but don't wash the oven. Add the butter, and warm over medium heat until the butter is melted. Pour in the egg mixture, and sprinkle the crumbled bacon over the top.

5 Arrange the apple slices on top of the egg mixture. Sprinkle the remaining ½ cup of Cheddar cheese over the top. Bake for about 20 minutes, until the eggs are set and the top is golden brown.

6 Remove from the oven and run a knife or flexible spatula around the edge of the frittata to loosen it. Carefully invert the frittata onto a cutting board. Slice into wedges and serve warm or at room temperature.

Chilaquiles with Eggs and Chipotles

SERVES 6 · PREP: 5 MINUTES · COOK: 25 MINUTES

ONE POT

2 tablespoons vegetable oil
   or olive oil

1 to 2 minced chipotle
   chiles, plus 1 to
   2 tablespoons sauce
   from a can or jar of
   chipotles in adobo

6 cups (about 5 ounces)
   thick-cut tortilla chips

3 cups fresh salsa

6 large eggs

¾ cup shredded Mexican
   queso fresco or Cheddar
   or Monterey Jack cheese

OPTIONAL GARNISHES

1 large avocado, sliced

½ cup sour cream

½ cup chopped cilantro

½ cup sliced scallions

1 lime, cut into wedges

Chilaquiles is a Mexican dish designed to transform last night's leftovers into a delicious, spicy breakfast. Traditionally, leftover corn tortillas are cut into strips and deep-fried, then tossed with salsa and leftover meat and vegetables, topped with cheese, and baked. This short-cut version uses tortilla chips, but you could certainly fry your own if you are so inclined. Serve any of the optional garnishes alongside, and let guests add their own.

1 Preheat the oven to 375°F.

2 In the Dutch oven, heat the oil over medium heat. Add the minced chipotle and sauce. Add the chips, breaking them up a bit in your hands. Cook, stirring, for 2 minutes, then add the salsa. Spread the mixture out into an even layer in the pot and make six wells or divots. Crack an egg into each well.

3 Bake, uncovered, for 12 to 15 minutes, until the whites of the eggs are fully set and the yolks are still a bit runny.

4 Sprinkle the cheese over the top and return to the oven to bake for about 5 minutes more, until the cheese has melted.

5 Cut into wedges with an egg in each wedge. Add garnishes as desired and serve.

Did You Know? Chipotle chiles are dried and smoked jalapeño chiles. You can find them in cans or jars, packed in adobo sauce—a tangy, sweet tomato sauce—in the international foods aisle of many supermarkets or at Mexican grocers. If you can't find them, substitute ½ teaspoon of ground chipotle or regular chili powder.

Savory Mushroom and Brie Bread Pudding

SERVES 8 · PREP: 15 MINUTES, PLUS 2 HOURS TO OVERNIGHT TO CHILL · COOK: 1 HOUR & 40 MINUTES

2 tablespoons olive oil

1 large shallot, minced

1 garlic clove, minced

1 pound mushrooms, such as button, cremini, or shiitake, sliced

1 tablespoon fresh thyme leaves

2 teaspoons kosher salt, divided

½ cup dry white wine

9 large eggs, lightly beaten

2 cups whole milk

1 cup heavy cream

2 tablespoons Dijon mustard

1 teaspoon freshly ground black pepper

1 pound day-old or toasted French bread, cut into cubes

1 (8-ounce) wheel or wedge of Brie cheese, top and bottom rinds cut off and discarded, cut into ½-inch cubes

¼ cup freshly grated Parmesan cheese

This savory bread pudding is hearty and comforting— as a bread pudding should be—but creamy Brie and sautéed mushrooms make it elegant enough for a festive occasion. The best part is, you can prep it the night before and simply pop it in the oven in the morning.

1 In the Dutch oven, heat the oil over medium-high heat. Add the shallot and cook, stirring frequently, until softened, about 3 minutes. Stir in the garlic and then the mushrooms, thyme, and ½ teaspoon of salt. Cook, stirring occasionally, until the mushrooms soften and begin to brown, about 8 minutes. Increase the heat to high and pour in the wine to deglaze the pot. Bring to a boil and cook, stirring and scraping up any browned bits from the bottom of the pot, until the liquid has evaporated, about 4 minutes. Remove from the heat and transfer the mushroom mixture to a bowl.

2 In a large bowl, whisk together the eggs, milk, cream, mustard, remaining 1½ teaspoons of salt, and pepper.

3 Add half of the bread cubes to the Dutch oven and spread them out into an even layer. Top with half of the mushroom mixture and half of the Brie. Top with the remaining bread cubes, the remaining mushroom mixture, and then the remaining Brie. Pour the egg mixture evenly over the top and press down gently to make sure that all the bread is saturated. Cover and refrigerate for 2 hours to overnight.

4 Preheat the oven to 350°F. Let the bread pudding stand at room temperature for 15 minutes before baking.

5 Bake the bread pudding, covered, for 60 minutes. Uncover, top with the Parmesan cheese, and bake for an additional 20 to 25 minutes, until the top is puffed and golden brown. Let cool for 10 to 15 minutes before serving.

Mediterranean Vegetable Strata

SERVES 8 • PREP: 20 MINUTES, PLUS 2 HOURS TO CHILL • COOK: 1 HOUR & 15 MINUTES

3 tablespoons olive oil

1 onion, diced

4 scallions, sliced

1 medium zucchini, diced

3 red or orange bell peppers, cut into thin strips

1 teaspoon kosher salt, plus a pinch

½ teaspoon freshly ground black pepper, plus a pinch

1 pound day-old or toasted French or Italian bread, cut into cubes

2 cups (about 8 ounces) crumbled feta cheese

1 cup freshly grated Parmesan cheese

12 large eggs

2½ cups whole milk

½ cup pitted and drained Kalamata olives

This comforting layered casserole is perfect for brunch, lunch, or dinner. It can be prepped the night before and cooked in the morning, making it a great party dish.

1 In the Dutch oven, heat the oil over medium-high heat. Add the onion and cook, stirring frequently, until softened, about 5 minutes. Reduce the heat to medium-low and add the scallions, zucchini, bell peppers, a pinch of salt, and a pinch of pepper. Cook, stirring, until the vegetables are tender and beginning to brown, about 10 minutes. Remove from the heat and transfer the vegetable mixture to a bowl.

2 Arrange half of the bread cubes in the Dutch oven, spreading them out into an even layer. Top with half of the vegetables, half of the feta, and half of the Parmesan cheese. Repeat this step with the remaining bread cubes, vegetables, and cheese.

3 In a large bowl, whisk together the eggs, milk, olives, remaining 1 teaspoon of salt, and remaining ½ teaspoon of pepper. Pour the egg mixture evenly over the bread, pressing down gently to make sure all the bread gets saturated. Cover and chill for at least 2 hours.

4 Preheat the oven to 350°F and let the strata stand at room temperature for 15 minutes before baking. Bake, uncovered, for about 60 minutes, or until the top of the strata is puffed and golden brown. Let stand for 10 to 15 minutes before serving.

Oven-Baked Tomato, Olive, and Feta Frittata

SERVES 6 • PREP: 5 MINUTES • COOK: 40 MINUTES

ONE POT

2 tablespoons olive oil

1 red bell pepper, seeded and diced

1 garlic clove, minced

10 large eggs

1 cup crumbled feta cheese

¼ cup water

2 tablespoons breadcrumbs

½ teaspoon kosher salt

¼ teaspoon freshly ground black pepper

1 tablespoon minced fresh oregano, plus additional leaves for garnish

1 tablespoon minced fresh basil, plus additional leaves for garnish

½ cup sliced black olives, such as kalamata

1 large tomato, diced

This simple frittata is full of the bright Mediterranean flavors of olives, tomatoes, feta cheese, and fresh herbs. It keeps well and is delicious served cold or at room temperature, so the leftovers are great for quick grab-and-go breakfasts or packed lunches.

1 Preheat the oven to 350°F.

2 In a Dutch oven, heat the oil over medium-high heat. Add the bell pepper and garlic and cook, stirring occasionally, until the peppers begin to soften, about 4 minutes.

3 In a large bowl, whisk together the eggs, feta, water, breadcrumbs, salt, pepper, oregano, and basil.

4 Add the tomatoes and olives to the Dutch oven and stir to combine with the peppers. Poor the egg mixture over the vegetables, stirring. Transfer the Dutch oven to the preheated oven and bake until lightly browned around the edges and set in the middle, about 35 to 40 minutes. Slice into wedges and serve, garnished with the remaining basil and oregano, if desired.

Bulgur Pilaf with Tomatoes and Mint (page 55)

Chapter Three

Appetizers & Sides

Warm Herbed Goat Cheese Dip in Mini Cocottes

MAKES ABOUT 3 CUPS • PREP: 10 MINUTES • COOK: 20 MINUTES

Butter or oil for preparing the mini cocottes

5 ounces goat cheese, at room temperature

2 ounces cream cheese, at room temperature

2 ounces Greek yogurt, at room temperature

½ cup grated Gruyère cheese, divided

1 tablespoon olive oil

1½ teaspoons balsamic vinegar

1 tablespoon minced flat-leaf parsley

1 teaspoon minced fresh sage

1 teaspoon minced fresh thyme

2 garlic cloves, minced

Kosher salt

Freshly ground black pepper

Baguette, pita chips, crackers, or vegetables, for dipping

This dip is quick and easy to make, looks great served in the mini cocottes it is cooked in, and is always a huge hit at parties. Tangy with goat cheese, loaded with fresh herbs and garlic, and heated to bubbly perfection, it's the perfect starter dish to serve on a cool evening.

1 Preheat the oven to 375°F and coat two 12-ounce mini cocottes with butter or oil. Set aside.

2 In a medium bowl, combine the goat cheese, cream cheese, yogurt, ¼ cup of Gruyère cheese, olive oil, vinegar, parsley, thyme, and garlic. Stir until well combined. Season with salt and pepper.

3 Spoon the cheese mixture into the prepared cocottes, dividing equally, and top with the remaining ¼ cup of Gruyère cheese. Bake for about 20 minutes, until the dip is bubbly and golden brown on top.

4 Serve hot with sliced baguette, pita chips, crackers, or vegetables for dipping.

Savory Wild Mushroom and Caramelized Onion Tartlets in Mini Cocottes

SERVES 4 • PREP: 10 MINUTES • COOK: 30 MINUTES

1 (16-ounce) package
   frozen puff pastry
   sheets, thawed

2 tablespoons
   unsalted butter

1 onion, thinly sliced

1½ tablespoons sugar

¼ cup balsamic vinegar

Kosher salt

Freshly ground
   black pepper

3 large eggs

⅔ cup half-and-half

8 ounces mixed wild
   mushrooms, chopped

1 tablespoon minced
   fresh sage

¼ cup finely grated
   Parmesan cheese

These savory custard-filled mini tarts make a memorable appetizer, and they can even be the centerpiece of a light vegetarian meal. The high heat of the cast iron cocottes ensures that the crust becomes perfectly crispy.

1 Preheat the oven to 400°F.

2 Lay the pastry sheets on a cutting board and cut out four circles, each about 1 inch larger in diameter than the 12-ounce cocottes. Press one circle into each of the four mini cocottes, covering the bottom and partway up the sides. Refrigerate until ready to fill.

3 In a medium skillet, melt the butter over medium-high heat. Add the onion and cook, stirring frequently, until softened, about 5 minutes. Stir in the sugar and vinegar and bring to a boil. Cook until the liquid has evaporated, then season with salt and pepper.

4 In a medium bowl, whisk together the eggs and half-and-half. Stir in the mushrooms and sage and season with salt and pepper.

5 Pour the onion mixture and the egg mixture into the mini cocottes, dividing equally. Bake for about 20 minutes, until the filling is set and the pastry is puffed and golden.

6 Sprinkle the Parmesan cheese over the tops of the tarts and place under the broiler for about 2 minutes, until the tops are golden. Serve immediately.

Saffron and Fontina Arancini

MAKES ABOUT 16 ARANCINI • PREP: 15 MINUTES • COOK: 50 MINUTES

FOR THE RISOTTO

2 tablespoons olive oil

1 medium shallot, diced

1 cup Arborio rice

¼ cup white wine

Pinch of saffron threads

4 cups chicken broth,
    heated and kept warm in
    a saucepan on the stove

½ cup grated
    Parmesan cheese

½ cup grated fontina cheese

Kosher salt

Freshly ground
    black pepper

FOR THE ARANCINI

Vegetable oil, for frying

½ cup all-purpose flour

2 large eggs, beaten

1 cup herbed bread crumbs

Arancini are deep-fried cheese-laced risotto balls . . . so make a double batch. They are a great way to use up leftover risotto, but these are made from scratch. After all, deep-frying and making risotto are two of the Dutch oven's special talents, and this recipe highlights both of them. A pinch of saffron adds an earthy flavor that mingles beautifully with the cheeses. If desired, serve them with marinara sauce for dipping.

TO MAKE THE RISOTTO

1 In the Dutch oven, heat the oil over medium-high heat. Add the shallot and cook, stirring frequently, until softened, about 3 minutes.

2 Stir in the rice until it is coated with the oil. Add the wine and cook, stirring, until most of the liquid has evaporated. Stir in the saffron.

3 Add the hot chicken broth, about ½ cup at a time, stirring after each addition until the broth is absorbed. Once all the broth has been incorporated, remove from the heat, stir in the Parmesan and fontina cheeses, and season with salt and pepper. Transfer the risotto to a bowl and set aside until cool enough to handle. >>

TO MAKE THE ARANCINI

1 Meanwhile, wash and dry the Dutch oven and then pour about 3 inches of vegetable oil into it. Heat the oil over medium-high heat until the temperature registers 350°F on a deep-fry thermometer. Line a plate with paper towels.

2 Form the risotto into 1½-inch balls. One at a time, roll the balls in the flour, then dunk them in the egg, and roll them in the bread crumbs. Fry the balls, several at a time, being careful not to crowd the pan, until golden brown all over, about 2 minutes per side. Drain on the prepared plate and serve hot.

Essential Technique: Very hot oil is crucial for making arancini that are crisp, golden brown, and not greasy. If you don't already have one, invest in a simple, inexpensive deep-fry thermometer and use it to make sure your oil reaches 350°F and stays near there the whole time you are frying your rice balls.

Barbecue Baked Beans with Bacon

SERVES 10 TO 12 • PREP: 10 MINUTES • COOK: 2 HOURS & 20 MINUTES

ONE POT

1 tablespoon vegetable oil

1 large onion, chopped

2 garlic cloves, minced

1½ cups ketchup

½ cup (packed) light
    brown sugar

½ cup light molasses

½ cup whole-grain mustard

¼ cup Worcestershire sauce

1 tablespoon hot
    pepper sauce

2 cups water

Kosher salt

Freshly ground
    black pepper

3 (15-ounce) cans navy or
    great northern beans,
    drained and rinsed

6 slices bacon, halved
    crosswise

These classic barbecue-style baked beans are sweet, smoky, and a bit spicy—the perfect match for barbecued ribs or chicken, but they are also delicious on their own. The Dutch oven expertly moves from the stove top to the oven for a perfectly seasoned, slow-baked pot of irresistible beans.

1 Preheat the oven to 350°F.

2 In the Dutch oven, heat the oil over high heat. Add the onion and garlic and cook, stirring frequently, until softened, about 5 minutes. Reduce the heat to low. Stir in the ketchup, brown sugar, molasses, mustard, Worcestershire sauce, hot pepper sauce, and water. Season with salt and pepper. Bring to a simmer and cook for 10 to 15 minutes, until the sauce thickens.

3 Add the beans, and lay the bacon slices on top in a single layer. Cover and bake for about 2 hours, until the liquid is bubbly and thickened. Serve hot.

Make It a Meal: Crisp, tangy coleslaw and meaty barbecued pork ribs are all you need to round out this meal. A side of Honey-Jalapeño Cornbread (page 181) would make a great accompaniment as well.

Mini Herb and Gruyère Soufflés in Mini Cocottes

SERVES 6 • PREP: 15 MINUTES • COOK: 30 MINUTES

4 tablespoons unsalted butter, plus additional at room temperature for preparing the cocottes

½ cup freshly grated Parmesan cheese, divided

5 tablespoons all-purpose flour

Pinch of cayenne pepper

Pinch of ground nutmeg

1 ¼ cups whole milk

¼ cup dry white wine

2 tablespoons minced chives

2 tablespoons minced flat-leaf parsley

6 large egg yolks (save the whites in a separate bowl)

1 teaspoon kosher salt

¼ teaspoon freshly ground black pepper

1 ¼ cups plus 2 tablespoons (about 6 ounces) grated Gruyère cheese, divided

8 large egg whites (use the 6 saved from separating the yolks, plus 2 additional)

Soufflés are plagued by myths and hearsay, scaring many a home cook off from attempting them. The truth is, they're pretty simple to make and always a dazzling dish to serve to guests. This savory version with strongly flavored Gruyère cheese, chives, and parsley could also be modified by varying the cheese used, adding different herbs or other ingredients, or even sweetening it up for dessert.

1 Preheat the oven to 400°F and generously coat six 10- or 12-ounce mini cocottes with butter. Sprinkle ¼ cup of Parmesan cheese inside the cocottes, dividing equally, to coat. Place the prepared mini cocottes on a rimmed baking sheet.

2 In a large saucepan set over medium heat, melt the 4 tablespoons butter. Whisk in the flour, cayenne, and nutmeg. Cook, whisking constantly, about 1 minute, until the mixture bubbles. Slowly whisk in the milk and then the wine, and cook, whisking constantly, until the mixture becomes smooth and thick and just begins to boil, about 2 minutes. Remove from the heat and stir in the herbs.

3 In a small bowl, whisk together the egg yolks, salt, and pepper. Add the egg mixture to the sauce, mixing quickly until well combined. Stir in 1¼ cups of Gruyère cheese and the remaining ¼ cup of Parmesan cheese.

4 In a large bowl using an electric mixer or in a stand mixer, beat the egg whites on high speed until stiff peaks form. Gently fold one-quarter of the whipped whites into the warm sauce mixture, then fold in the remaining whites. Spoon the soufflé mixture into the prepared cocottes. Sprinkle the remaining 2 tablespoons of Gruyère cheese over the tops. Wipe the rims clean.

5 Transfer the cocottes on the baking sheet to the oven. Reduce the heat to 375°F and bake for about 25 minutes, until the soufflés are golden brown and puffed. Serve immediately.

Essential Technique: The keys to lofty soufflés are to whip the egg whites until stiff and to fold them gently into the other ingredients so as to maintain as much of the airiness you've whipped into them as possible. If the tops are browning too quickly, place a piece of aluminum foil over the tops and continue to cook until the center is set.

Curried Corn Fritters with Cilantro and Mint Chutney

MAKES ABOUT 30 (2-INCH) FRITTERS • PREP: 15 MINUTES • COOK: 30 MINUTES

FOR THE CHUTNEY

2 cups (packed) cilantro sprigs

1 cup (packed) fresh mint leaves

½ small onion, chopped

¼ cup water

1 tablespoon freshly squeezed lime juice

½ to 1 fresh green chile, such as serrano or jalapeño, or to taste

1 teaspoon sugar

Made with fresh corn folded into a curry-spiced batter, these piquant fritters are fried until crisp and golden brown and served with a spicy and flavorful cilantro and mint sauce for dunking. The Spicy Mango Chutney on page 63 would be a nice additional or alternative accompaniment. If fear of making a huge mess on your stove top has kept you from deep-frying, this is a great recipe to help you get over it. The high sides of the Dutch oven contain the splatter nicely, and these spicy corn fritters are well worth any extra effort.

TO MAKE THE CHUTNEY

In a blender or food processor, combine the cilantro, mint, onion, water, lime juice, chile, and sugar, and process until mostly smooth.

TO MAKE THE FRITTERS

1 In the Dutch oven, heat the oil over medium-high heat until the temperature registers 360°F on a deep-fry thermometer. Line a plate with paper towels.

FOR THE FRITTERS

2 quarts peanut or
    vegetable oil, for frying

¾ cup all-purpose flour

½ cup medium-ground
    cornmeal

2 teaspoons baking powder

1 tablespoon curry powder

¾ teaspoon kosher salt

¼ teaspoon cayenne pepper

¾ cup whole milk

1 large egg

4 ears white or yellow corn,
    shucked and kernels cut
    from the cob

5 scallions, white and
    light green parts only,
    thinly sliced

2 In a large bowl, whisk together the flour, cornmeal, baking powder, curry powder, salt, and cayenne.

3 In a small bowl or measuring cup, whisk together the milk and egg.

4 Add the egg mixture to the flour mixture and stir to mix well. Add the corn kernels and scallions and stir to incorporate.

5 Once the oil is hot, drop the batter by the heaping tablespoonful into the oil, being careful not to crowd the pot. Cook, turning once or twice, until the fritters are golden brown all around, about 4 minutes. Using tongs, a slotted spoon, or a spider, transfer the fritters to the prepared plate as they are finished cooking. Repeat until all the batter has been cooked.

6 Serve hot with the chutney alongside for dipping.

Essential Technique: Use a deep-frying thermometer to monitor the oil's temperature. If it's not hot enough, your fritters will cook slowly and absorb too much oil, making them greasy. If it's too hot, the fritters will burn.

Wild Rice Pilaf with Pistachios and Raisins

SERVES 8 • PREP: 10 MINUTES • COOK: 50 MINUTES

ONE POT

2 tablespoons
    unsalted butter

1 tablespoon vegetable oil

3 large shallots, minced

2 cups wild rice

4 cups chicken or
    vegetable broth

½ cup raisins

1 bay leaf

2 sprigs fresh thyme sprigs

½ teaspoon kosher salt

⅛ teaspoon freshly ground
    black pepper

½ cup coarsely chopped
    pistachios

¼ cup minced
    flat-leaf parsley

Wild rice has a toothsome, chewy texture and a delicious nutty flavor. Here it is cooked with savory broth and sweet raisins. First, shallots are sautéed in the Dutch oven on the stove top, then the rice and other ingredients are added. The prep time is short, so while the dish is baking in the oven, you can attend to your other dishes.

1 Preheat the oven to 375°F.

2 In the Dutch oven, heat the butter with the oil over medium-high heat. Add the shallots and cook, stirring frequently, until softened, about 3 minutes. Stir in the rice until the grains are coated with the oil. Add the broth, raisins, bay leaf, thyme, salt, and pepper, and bring to a simmer.

3 Cover and bake for about 45 minutes, until the rice is tender and the liquid has been absorbed.

4 Remove the bay leaf and thyme sprigs and discard them. Stir in the pistachios and parsley and serve hot.

Make It a Meal: Serve this sweet, savory pilaf alongside Middle Eastern–spiced grilled meats or fish, and zucchini sautéed with garlic.

Bulgur Pilaf with Tomatoes and Mint

SERVES 6 + PREP: 10 MINUTES + COOK: 30 MINUTES

ONE POT

2 tablespoons olive oil

1 onion, diced

1 garlic clove, minced

1-inch piece fresh
    ginger, minced

1½ cups bulgur

½ teaspoon ground turmeric

½ teaspoon ground cumin

2 cups vegetable or
    chicken broth

1 (14.5-ounce) can diced
    tomatoes, drained

1 cup diced eggplant

1 teaspoon kosher salt

½ cup (loosely packed)
    finely chopped
    fresh mint

¼ cup (loosely packed)
    finely chopped
    flat-leaf parsley

Juice of 1 lemon

Bulgur makes a welcome change from rice. It's slightly chewy, with a subtle nutty flavor. Paired with fresh mint, tomatoes, and lemon, it is a perfect side for grilled fish or meat. Add a can of chickpeas, some diced tofu, or raw shrimp a few minutes before it's finished cooking, and you'll have a healthy and delicious one-pot meal.

1 In the Dutch oven, heat the oil over medium heat. Add the onion and cook, stirring frequently, until softened and beginning to brown, about 7 minutes.

2 Add the garlic and ginger and cook, stirring, for 1 more minute. Stir in the bulgur, turmeric, and cumin and cook, stirring, for 1 minute.

3 Add the broth, tomatoes, eggplant, and salt and bring to a boil. Reduce the heat to medium-low, cover, and simmer for about 15 minutes, until the liquid has been fully absorbed. Remove the pot from the heat and let stand, covered and without stirring, for 5 minutes.

4 Just before serving, stir in the mint, parsley, and lemon juice and serve hot.

Did You Know? Bulgur is wheat berries that have been parboiled, dried, and cracked. Cracked wheat is raw wheat berries that have been cracked but not parboiled, so it needs a much longer cooking time than bulgur.

Oven-Baked Polenta with Sweet Corn Aioli

SERVES 8 • PREP: 10 MINUTES • COOK: 1 HOUR

FOR THE POLENTA

Butter or oil for preparing the Dutch oven

2 cups dry polenta (coarsely ground yellow cornmeal)

2 cups sweet corn kernels, fresh (from about 2 ears) or frozen

2 garlic cloves, minced

2 teaspoons kosher salt

1 teaspoon freshly ground black pepper

7 cups chicken or vegetable broth or water

1 cup grated Parmesan cheese, plus additional for serving

½ cup heavy cream

4 tablespoons unsalted butter

Like risotto, polenta is easy to cook, but most recipes require the cook to stand at the stove, whisking constantly, until the dry cornmeal turns to a rich, smooth texture by absorbing the liquid. For this version, I mix the cornmeal and liquid in the Dutch oven and then bake the mixture, completely hands free, for nearly an hour, during which I can focus on cooking the rest of the meal—or better yet, relax with a glass of wine and some good conversation.

TO MAKE THE POLENTA

1 Preheat the oven to 350°F and coat the inside of the Dutch oven with butter or oil.

2 In the Dutch oven, combine the polenta, corn, garlic, salt, and pepper. Add the broth and stir to mix.

3 Bake, uncovered, for 50 minutes. Stir in the Parmesan cheese, cream, and butter, and return to the oven. Bake for an additional 10 minutes. >>

FOR THE AIOLI

2 garlic cloves

2 teaspoons Dijon mustard

3 egg yolks

2 tablespoons fresh
    lemon juice

Kosher salt

1 cup neutral-flavored
    oil, such as grapeseed,
    safflower, or sunflower
    seed oil

2 cups fresh corn kernels

TO MAKE THE AIOLI

1 While the polenta is baking, make the aioli. Chop the garlic in a food processor. Add the mustard, egg yolks, lemon juice, and a pinch of salt. Process for about 2 minutes, until the mixture is fully incorporated and pale yellow. With the motor running, slowly add the oil in a thin stream. Continue to process until the mixture is thick and creamy. Taste and add additional salt if needed. Transfer the mixture to a medium bowl and stir in the corn kernels.

2 To serve, cut the polenta into wedges and serve with the aioli for dipping.

Roasted Root Vegetables with Maple-Balsamic Glaze

SERVES 6 • PREP: 15 MINUTES • COOK: 55 MINUTES

4 small parsnips, peeled
   and cut on the bias
   into 2-inch lengths

3 small turnips, quartered

3 small gold beets, halved

3 small red beets, halved

2 leeks, halved lengthwise

1 red onion, cut into wedges

3 tablespoons olive oil

Kosher salt

Freshly ground
   black pepper

1 cup pure maple syrup

¼ cup balsamic vinegar

These earthy root vegetables are roasted to perfection in the Dutch oven and then drizzled with a sweet, savory balsamic glaze. They make a great accompaniment to roasted or grilled meats. Store any leftovers in the refrigerator and toss them into salads or sandwiches later in the week.

1 Preheat the oven to 425°F.

2 In the Dutch oven, toss together the parsnips, turnips, beets, leeks, and onion with the olive oil until well coated. Season with salt and pepper. Bake, uncovered, for 45 to 50 minutes, until the vegetables are tender.

3 Meanwhile, in a small saucepan, combine the maple syrup and vinegar and bring to a boil over medium-high heat. Reduce the heat to low and simmer until the mixture has reduced by about half and is thick and syrupy. Remove from the heat.

4 Once the vegetables are tender, drizzle the syrup over the top and return the pot to the oven to roast for another 5 minutes. Serve hot.

Essential Technique: The key to perfectly roasted vegetables is to choose varieties that all have similar cooking times. Root vegetables take longer to roast than more delicate veggies, like squash or peppers. These hearty vegetables can roast in a hot oven for close to an hour without being overcooked.

Baked Brie with Apples, Nuts, and Honey in Mini Cocottes

SERVES 4 • PREP: 10 MINUTES • COOK: 40 MINUTES

2 large crisp apples

1 (8-ounce) wheel or wedge of Brie cheese, top and bottom rinds cut off and discarded

½ cup chopped walnuts or pecans (or use a mixture)

2 tablespoons honey

Pinch of kosher salt

¼ teaspoon cinnamon

Bread or crackers, for serving

Creamy cheese, sweet honey and apples, and toasted nuts are made for one another. Though super quick from start to finish, this simple appetizer is surprisingly impressive. Serve it with crackers or sliced baguette to spread the apples and cheese on.

1 Preheat the oven to 375°F.

2 Cut the top quarter of the apples off so that you have a flat top. Scoop out the apple cores and then use a thin knife to make two concentric circular cuts around the cores, cutting almost but not all the way through the bottom of the apple. Turn the apple upside down so that it is resting on its flat cut surface. Make several slits in the apple starting about ½ inch below the bottom or stem end of the apple (so that the apple still holds together after the cuts are made).

3 Place each apple in a 10- or 12-inch mini cocotte, with the cut side up.

4 Split the Brie in half and place one half on top of each apple, pressing it down to shape it over the apple. Bake for 20 minutes.

5 Meanwhile, in a small saucepan set over medium heat, toast the nuts until they just begin to brown and release a nutty aroma. Stir in the honey, salt, and cinnamon, coating the nuts well.

6 Remove the cocottes from the oven and spoon the nut mixture over the tops of the apples, dividing equally. Bake for an additional 15 to 20 minutes, until the apples are tender.

7 Serve hot with bread or crackers.

Perfect Pairing: Serve glasses of a crisp sauvignon blanc or dry champagne or other sparkling wine with this sweet and creamy appetizer.

Bourbon-Spiked Cranberry Sauce

MAKES ABOUT 3 CUPS · PREP: 5 MINUTES · COOK: 30 MINUTES

1 pound (about 4 cups) cranberries

2 cups sugar

½ cup apple juice

¼ teaspoon ground cinnamon

¼ cup bourbon

This recipe is so simple that you'll never even consider buying the canned stuff again. This ever so slightly boozy cranberry sauce is the perfect side for your Thanksgiving turkey, but you can make it anytime to have on turkey sandwiches, roast chicken, or other meats.

1 In the Dutch oven, combine all the ingredients and bring to a boil, stirring frequently, over medium-high heat.

2 Reduce the heat to medium-low and simmer, stirring occasionally, for 25 to 30 minutes, until the sauce thickens and the cranberries begin to break down. Cool before serving.

Spicy Mango Chutney

MAKES ABOUT 2½ CUPS • PREP: 10 MINUTES • COOK: 25 MINUTES

2 medium apples, peeled, cored, and chopped

1 large mango, seeded, peeled, and chopped

1 hot red chile, seeded and diced

¾ cup sugar

½ small onion, diced

¼ cup golden raisins

¼ cup white vinegar

2 tablespoons finely chopped, peeled fresh ginger

2 teaspoons freshly squeezed lemon juice

1 teaspoon curry powder

¼ teaspoon cinnamon

¼ teaspoon ground nutmeg

¼ teaspoon kosher salt

This spicy, sweet chutney is the perfect accompaniment to all sorts of Indian curries as well as grilled or roasted meats. It also makes a divine spread for a grilled cheese sandwich made with extra-sharp Cheddar cheese, or even on a plain piece of toast.

1 In the Dutch oven, combine the apples, mango, chile, sugar, onion, raisins, vinegar, and ginger and set over high heat. Bring the mixture to a boil and then reduce the heat and simmer, stirring occasionally, until the fruit softens and the liquid thickens, about 20 minutes. Stir in the lemon juice, curry powder, cinnamon, nutmeg, and salt and continue to boil for another 5 minutes.

2 Remove from the heat and cool before serving.

Beef Chili with Butternut
Squash (page 84)

Chapter Four

Soups & Stews

French Onion Soup with Gruyère Toasts in Mini Cocottes

SERVES 4 • PREP: 10 MINUTES • COOK: 45 MINUTES

6 tablespoons unsalted butter, divided

3 onions, 2½ chopped, ½ cut into ⅛-inch-thick rounds

2 cups beef broth

1 bay leaf

3 sprigs fresh thyme

2 teaspoons white wine vinegar

Kosher salt

Freshly ground black pepper

4 slices crusty bread, cut into rounds slightly larger than the cocottes

¾ cup grated Gruyère cheese

French onion soup is a classic dish that always makes a great starter on a cold night. The onions are first cooked slowly in butter until their sugars are beautifully caramelized, giving the soup its distinctive rich flavor. A layer of cheesy toast is the perfect crowning touch.

1 Preheat the oven to 400°F.

2 In the Dutch oven, melt 2 tablespoons of the butter over medium-high heat. Add the chopped onions and reduce the heat to medium-low. Cook, stirring occasionally, until the onions are softened and browned, about 20 minutes.

3 Stir in the broth, bay leaf, thyme, and vinegar. Season with salt and pepper. Simmer for 10 minutes. Remove and discard the bay leaf and thyme sprigs.

4 Ladle the soup into four mini cocottes, dividing equally.

5 In a skillet, heat the remaining 4 tablespoons of butter over medium-high heat. Fry the onion rounds until browned on both sides, about 5 minutes total. Remove the onions and fry the bread slices until browned on both sides, about 4 minutes. Place a toasted bread round on top of each cocotte, top with an onion round, and then sprinkle the Gruyère cheese over the top. Bake until the cheese is melted and bubbly, about 4 minutes. Serve hot.

Creamy Cauliflower Soup with Stilton and Pears

SERVES 4 • PREP: 10 MINUTES • COOK: 30 MINUTES

ONE POT

WEEKNIGHT WIN

2 tablespoons butter

2 shallots, diced

1 celery stalk, diced

2 Bosc pears, peeled, cored, and chopped

1 head cauliflower, broken into florets

2 cups vegetable broth

2 tablespoons crème fraîche or heavy cream

4 ounces Stilton cheese, roughly chopped, plus additional for garnish

2 tablespoons chopped flat-leaf parsley, plus additional for garnish

Kosher salt

Freshly ground black pepper

¼ cup chopped, toasted walnuts

This creamy soup is delicately flavored with cauliflower and pears. The blue cheese adds a sharp, salty bite. The walnuts are the perfect finishing touch, adding a bit of crunch and a nice hint of nutty flavor.

1 In the Dutch oven, melt the butter over medium-high heat. Add the shallots and celery and cook, stirring frequently, until softened, about 5 minutes. Add the pears and cauliflower, stirring to mix. Add the broth and bring to a boil. Reduce the heat to medium-low and simmer for about 20 minutes, until the cauliflower is softened.

2 Add the crème fraîche, Stilton cheese, and parsley and simmer for 5 minutes more. Remove from the heat and blend until smooth using an immersion blender, or in batches in a countertop blender. Taste and season with salt and pepper.

3 Serve the soup hot, garnished with the walnuts, additional Stilton cheese, and additional parsley.

Essential Technique: To toast the walnuts, preheat the oven to 350°F. Spread the nuts in a single layer in a shallow pan or rimmed baking sheet. Bake for about 5 minutes, until they turn golden brown. Watch them carefully to make sure they don't burn.

Ribollita

SERVES 6 TO 8 • PREP: 10 MINUTES • COOK: 40 MINUTES

ONE POT

2 tablespoons olive oil, plus
   additional for garnish

4 ounces pancetta,
   diced (optional)

4 garlic cloves, minced

1 medium onion, diced

2 medium carrots,
   peeled and diced

2 large celery ribs, diced

1 bay leaf

¾ teaspoon kosher salt

½ teaspoon freshly ground
   black pepper, plus
   additional for seasoning

10 ounces Tuscan kale, thick
   center stems removed,
   leaves julienned

6 cups vegetable or
   chicken broth

1 (14½-ounce) can
   diced tomatoes

2 tablespoons tomato paste

2 (14½-ounce) cans
   cannellini beans,
   drained and rinsed

8 to 10 slices day-old crusty
   bread, torn into pieces

Freshly grated Parmesan
   cheese, for serving

Ribollita is a classic soup that has been made in Tuscany for centuries. Its defining features are that it includes tomatoes, greens, white beans, and stale bread. The bread makes it heartier than your typical vegetable soup. Pancetta adds a layer of good, meaty flavor, but feel free to leave it out. Ribollita is even better the next day, so make a big pot of it today and you'll have tomorrow night's dinner taken care of, too.

1 In the Dutch oven, heat the oil over medium-high heat. Add the pancetta (if using) and cook, stirring frequently, until the pancetta is crisp, about 3 minutes.

2 Add the garlic, onion, carrots, celery, bay leaf, salt, and pepper and cook, stirring frequently, for about 5 minutes, until the vegetables have softened.

3 Stir in the kale and cook for about 3 minutes more. Add the broth, tomatoes, and tomato paste.

4 In a small bowl, combine ¼ cup of beans with a bit of the broth from the soup and mash the beans into a paste. Stir the paste and the remaining beans into the soup and bring to a boil. Reduce the heat to medium-low and simmer, uncovered, until the beans and vegetables are tender, about 25 minutes. Remove and discard the bay leaf.

5 To serve, place a few pieces of bread in each serving bowl and ladle the soup over the top. Serve hot, seasoned with freshly ground black pepper. Serve with Parmesan cheese and a drizzle of olive oil, if desired.

Matzo Ball Soup

SERVES 6 • PREP: 15 MINUTES • COOK: 1 HOUR

2 large eggs, lightly beaten

½ cup matzo meal

2 tablespoons water

2 teaspoons salt, divided

4 tablespoons olive oil, divided

1 onion, diced

1 garlic clove, minced

2 large carrots, peeled and cut into rounds

1 large parsnip, peeled and cut into rounds

2 celery stalks, diced

½ teaspoon freshly ground black pepper

8 cups chicken broth

3 cups diced cooked chicken

2 tablespoons minced fresh dill, plus additional for garnish (optional)

Matzo ball soup isn't just for Passover in my house. In fact, more often than not, when I ask my son to choose what's for dinner, this is his pick. When I'm feeling particularly industrious, I cook a whole chicken, take the meat off the bones, make homemade stock, and proceed with the recipe from there. But more often I use leftover roast chicken or even a rotisserie chicken from the market and store-bought broth. I'm convinced that the parsnip is the secret ingredient that makes this soup taste like a Jewish grandmother made it.

1 In a medium bowl, combine the eggs, matzo meal, water, 1 teaspoon of salt, and 2 tablespoons of olive oil. Mix well. Cover and refrigerate for 20 minutes.

2 In a Dutch oven, heat the remaining 2 tablespoons of olive oil over medium-high heat. Add the onion and garlic and cook, stirring, until softened, about 5 minutes. Add the carrots, parsnip, celery, the remaining teaspoon of salt, the pepper, and the broth and bring to a boil.

3 Reduce the heat to medium-low and cook, uncovered, stirring occasionally, for about 30 minutes, until the vegetables are tender.

4 While the soup is simmering, bring a separate large pot of lightly salted water to a boil. Reduce the heat to low. Form the matzo meal mixture into 1½-inch balls and drop them into the simmering water. Cover the pot and let simmer, undisturbed, for about 30 minutes. To test to see if the matzo balls are done, cut one in half. The inside should be uniform in appearance. Remove the matzo balls from the water with a slotted spoon.

5 Stir the chicken into the soup and cook for a few minutes more to heat through. Just before serving, stir in the dill (if using).

6 To serve, place a few matzo balls in each serving bowl and ladle the soup over the top. Garnish with the remaining dill (if using) and serve immediately.

Essential Technique: The trick to fluffy matzo balls is a light touch. Gently form the mixture into balls, being careful not to overhandle it, drop the balls into the simmering water, cover tightly, and let them cook undisturbed for 30 minutes before checking on them.

Lemony White Bean Stew with Chicken and Fresh Herb Pesto

SERVES 6 • PREP: 10 MINUTES, PLUS OVERNIGHT TO SOAK THE BEANS • COOK: 1 HOUR & 40 MINUTES

FOR THE CHICKEN AND BEANS

2 tablespoons olive oil

4 garlic cloves, minced

1 onion, diced

1 pound dried white beans, such as cannellini or flageolet, soaked in water overnight and drained

2 cups chicken broth

1 lemon

1 teaspoon kosher salt, plus additional to season the chicken

2 pounds boneless, skinless chicken thighs

Freshly ground black pepper

4 sprigs fresh thyme

This delicious and hearty stew is full of simple, bright flavors like lemon, dill, garlic, and mint. The beans need to be soaked overnight (see the Essential Technique tip, below, for a quick-soaking method), and the dish cooks in the oven for an hour and a half, but the hands-on time is extremely minimal. Some crusty bread and a crisp green salad make this a satisfying meal.

TO MAKE THE CHICKEN AND BEANS

1 Preheat the oven to 350°F.

2 In the Dutch oven, heat the oil over medium heat. Add the garlic and onion and cook, stirring frequently, until softened, about 5 minutes. Stir in the beans and remove from the heat. Add the broth and enough water to just barely cover the beans.

3 Using a vegetable peeler, shave off the yellow peel of the lemon, being careful to leave behind the bitter white pith. Juice the lemon and stir the lemon juice into the beans, along with the peel and 1 teaspoon of salt.

4 Season the chicken thighs with salt and pepper, then place them on top of the bean mixture and top with the thyme. Set the Dutch oven over high heat and bring to a simmer. Cover the Dutch oven and transfer it to the oven. Bake for about 1½ hours, until the beans are tender.

FOR THE PESTO

2 cups (packed) fresh
mint leaves

½ cup (packed) fresh dill

¼ cup pine nuts

Zest of 1 lemon

1 tablespoon freshly
squeezed lemon juice

1 garlic clove

2 tablespoons olive oil, plus
additional if needed

½ teaspoon kosher salt

Freshly ground
black pepper

FOR SERVING

1 lemon

4 ounces crumbled
feta cheese, for
serving (optional)

TO MAKE THE PESTO

In a food processor or blender, combine the mint, dill, pine nuts, lemon zest, lemon juice, garlic, olive oil, salt, and pepper and process until finely minced. Add additional oil, if needed, to achieve the desired consistency.

TO SERVE

1 Remove the Dutch oven from the oven and discard the thyme sprigs. Transfer the chicken to a bowl, and shred it. Stir in the lemon zest and lemon juice.

2 Serve the beans hot, topped with the shredded chicken, a dollop of the herb pesto, and a sprinkling of feta cheese (if using).

Essential Technique: If you've forgotten to soak your beans overnight, you can still pull off this recipe today. Rinse the beans and put them in your Dutch oven, covered with about 2 inches of water. Bring to a boil over high heat. Remove the pot from the heat, cover, and let the beans soak for 1 hour. Drain the beans and proceed with the recipe.

Smoked Pork Ramen Soup

SERVES 4 · PREP: 15 MINUTES · COOK: 15 MINUTES

ONE POT

WEEKNIGHT WIN

1 tablespoon grapeseed oil

1 pound smoked pork loin
   or roasted pork

8 scallions, sliced, white and
   green parts separated

1 (2-inch) piece fresh ginger,
   peeled and sliced

6 cups chicken broth

1 tablespoon mirin

1 tablespoon soy sauce

2 teaspoons rice wine
   vinegar

Kosher salt

Freshly ground
   black pepper

1½ pounds fresh ramen
   noodles (or substitute
   2 packages of instant
   ramen, discarding the
   seasoning packets),
   cooked according to
   package directions.

1 large carrot, grated

2 radishes, halved and
   thinly sliced

½ cup fresh cilantro leaves

Making ramen from scratch is a true art—and an endeavor that takes all day. This simple version cheats by using chicken broth instead of homemade pork stock. Fresh ramen noodles elevate it way above the packaged stuff you may be used to, but in a pinch, you can use the instant noodles from those packages and it's likely no one will notice.

1 In the Dutch oven, heat the oil over medium-high heat. Add the pork and cook, turning once, until browned on both sides, about 3 to 4 minutes. Remove it from the pot and let it rest.

2 Reduce the heat to low and add the scallion whites and ginger. Cook, stirring, for about 30 seconds, and then stir in the broth and mirin and bring to a boil. Add the soy sauce and vinegar. Simmer for 10 minutes. Taste and add salt and pepper, if needed.

3 To serve, slice the pork into ¼-inch-thick slices. Divide the noodles among four serving bowls and then ladle the hot broth over them. Top each bowl with a few slices of the pork and some of the carrot, radish slices, cilantro, and scallion greens. Serve hot.

Did You Know? Mirin is a sweet Japanese rice wine that is used for cooking. You can find it in the Asian foods aisle of most supermarkets, or substitute white wine, preferably one that is on the sweeter side.

Moroccan Chickpea Stew with Baby Mustard Greens

SERVES 4 • PREP: 10 MINUTES • COOK: 20 MINUTES

ONE POT

WEEKNIGHT WIN

2 large garlic cloves, crushed

1 teaspoon minced fresh ginger

½ teaspoon kosher salt

Pinch of saffron threads

2 teaspoons sweet paprika

1 teaspoon ground cumin

½ teaspoon coriander

¼ teaspoon cinnamon

¼ teaspoon cayenne pepper

Pinch of freshly ground black pepper

2 (15-ounce) cans chickpeas, with their liquid

4 tablespoons olive oil, divided

1 small onion, diced

1 large tomato, peeled, seeded, and chopped

1 cup water

¼ cup golden raisins

5 ounces baby mustard greens

Aromatic spices, sweet raisins, and a bit of heat flavor this North African–style vegetarian stew. Baby mustard greens add an herby, peppery note, but you could always substitute baby spinach or arugula if you can't find them. Serve this hearty stew with hunks of crusty bread for dipping.

1 Mash the garlic, ginger, salt, and saffron into a paste using either a mortar and pestle or the side of a large knife on a wooden cutting board.

2 In a small bowl, combine the garlic paste with the paprika, cumin, coriander, cinnamon, cayenne, and pepper and stir to combine. Add ¼ cup of liquid from the chickpea cans and stir to mix.

3 In the Dutch oven, heat 2 tablespoons of olive oil over medium-high heat. Add the onion and tomato and cook, stirring occasionally, until softened, about 4 minutes. Stir in the garlic paste mixture and cook for 1 minute more.

4 Add the chickpeas with their remaining liquid and the water to the Dutch oven. Stir in the raisins and bring to a boil. Reduce the heat to medium, stir in the greens, and simmer, uncovered, for 15 minutes.

5 Serve the stew hot, garnished with the remaining 2 tablespoons of olive oil.

Classic Fish Chowder

SERVES 8 · PREP: 10 MINUTES · COOK: 40 MINUTES

ONE POT

5 slices bacon, diced

1 large onion, diced

2 teaspoons kosher salt

¾ teaspoon freshly ground
    black pepper

2 tablespoons
    all-purpose flour

2 cups fish stock, chicken
    broth, or water

3 medium Yukon gold
    potatoes, cut into
    ½-inch pieces

⅓ cup heavy cream

1¾ cups whole milk

2 pounds white fish, such as
    cod, hake, or pollock, cut
    into 1-inch pieces

2 tablespoons chopped flat-
    leaf parsley, for garnish

New England–style fish chowder is rich, creamy, and thickened with potatoes. You can make it with just about any type of fish or shellfish. I like to use meaty cod or pollock, but you could substitute clams, scallops, shrimp, or a combination of any of these.

1 In the Dutch oven, cook the bacon over medium heat, stirring occasionally, until crisp, about 8 minutes. Using a slotted spoon, transfer half of the bacon to paper towels to drain. Drain most of the rendered fat, leaving 2 to 3 tablespoons in the pot.

2 Reduce the heat to medium-low and add the onion, salt, and pepper. Cook, stirring frequently, until the onion is softened and beginning to brown, 10 to 12 minutes.

3 Sprinkle the flour over the onion and cook, stirring, for 1 to 2 minutes. Slowly add the stock, stirring constantly, until the flour dissolves and the liquid begins to thicken.

4 Stir in the potatoes and cream, increase the heat to medium, cover, and simmer until the potatoes are tender, about 7 minutes. Reduce the heat to low and stir in the milk. Add the fish pieces and cook for about 5 minutes more, until the fish is opaque and cooked through.

5 Serve hot, garnished with the reserved bacon and parsley.

Make It a Meal: This recipe is a hearty meal in and of itself. Serve it with crusty bread and a crisp salad, and you're good to go.

Seafood Stew with Spanish Chorizo and Fennel

SERVES 4 • PREP: 10 MINUTES • COOK: 30 MINUTES

1 tablespoon olive oil, plus additional as needed

6 ounces chorizo, diced (Spanish) or removed from casing and crumbled (Mexican)

1 large fennel bulb, diced

1 onion, diced

4 garlic cloves, smashed and chopped

2 tablespoons tomato paste

1 cup dry white wine

4 cups chicken broth

2 medium tomatoes, diced

1 teaspoon fish sauce

Kosher salt

Freshly ground black pepper

8 ounces firm fish, such as cod, halibut, mahi mahi, or salmon

1 pound mussels

1 pound large prawns, peeled and deveined

1 lemon, for garnish

⅓ cup chopped flat-leaf parsley, for garnish

This light, summery seafood stew is quick and easy to make but is layered with deep, complex flavors. Chorizo gives the stew meaty and spicy flavors, caramelized fennel and onions add sweetness, and tomatoes provide a brilliant tang. You can use either Spanish chorizo, which is dried, cured, and mildly spiced, or Mexican chorizo, which is fresh, uncooked sausage that is heavily spiced.

1 In the Dutch oven, heat the olive oil over medium-high heat. Add the chorizo and cook, stirring frequently, until browned, about 5 minutes. Transfer the sausage to a paper towel–lined plate and remove all but 2 tablespoons of the fat from the Dutch oven. If you end up with less than 2 tablespoons of fat, add a bit of olive oil.

2 Add the fennel to the Dutch oven and cook, stirring frequently, for 3 minutes. Reduce the heat to medium, add the onion, and cook, stirring occasionally, until the vegetables are softened, about 8 minutes. Add the garlic and cook until the garlic begins to brown, about 2 minutes more.

3 Increase the heat to high, stir in the tomato paste and cook, stirring constantly, until the tomato paste begins to darken, about 3 minutes more.

4 Reduce the heat to medium-high, add the wine, and cook, stirring, until most of the liquid evaporates, about 2 minutes. Stir in the broth, tomatoes, chorizo, and fish sauce and bring to a simmer. Taste and add salt and pepper as needed.

5 Add the fish and let simmer for about 2 minutes. Stir in the mussels and prawns, cover, and cook for 5 to 6 minutes, until the mussels open (discard any that don't open), and the prawns turn opaque.

6 Ladle the broth, vegetables, fish, and shellfish into bowls, squeeze a bit of lemon juice over, and garnish with parsley. Serve hot.

Make It a Meal: All you need to make this stew a full meal is some crusty bread for dunking. Better yet, serve it with buttery garlic bread.

Shrimp and Andouille Sausage Gumbo

SERVES 4 TO 6 • PREP: 15 MINUTES • COOK: 1 HOUR

ONE POT

¼ cup vegetable oil

⅓ cup all-purpose flour

2 cups sliced okra

1 large onion, diced

1 red or green bell
pepper, diced

4 celery stalks, diced

4 garlic cloves, minced

2 tablespoons tomato paste

1 tablespoon chopped
fresh thyme

2 teaspoons paprika

½ teaspoon cayenne
pepper, or more
as seasoning

A classic gumbo always starts with a roux cooked slowly until brown and toasty. This roux thickens and flavors the broth. Okra also thickens the broth. Fresh okra can be hard to find, but most supermarkets carry frozen sliced okra. You can add it still frozen to the soup, though you will need to add a few minutes to the cooking time. Filé powder, found in the spice section of many supermarkets, is made from sassafras leaves. It adds flavor and thickness to gumbo.

1 In the Dutch oven, heat the oil over medium heat for about 5 minutes. Whisk in the flour and cook, whisking constantly, until the mixture turns chestnut brown and gives off a nutty aroma, lowering the heat if needed to prevent burning. This will take about 15 minutes.

2 Add the okra and cook, stirring, until it softens and any sliminess disappears, about 5 minutes.

1 teaspoon kosher salt

½ teaspoon freshly ground
black pepper

1 cup canned diced
tomatoes or 1 large
tomato, diced

6 ounces Andouille
sausage, cut into
1-inch-thick slices

6 cups chicken broth

1 pound shrimp, peeled
and deveined

1 tablespoon filé
powder (optional)

Steamed white rice,
for serving

Scallions, white and light
green parts only, thinly
sliced, for garnish

3 Add the onion, bell pepper, and celery and cook, stirring, over medium heat for about 5 minutes, until the vegetables have softened.

4 Stir in the garlic and then add the tomato paste, thyme, paprika, cayenne, salt, and pepper. Stir in the tomatoes and sausage and cook for 2 minutes more.

5 Add the broth and stir well, scraping up any browned bits from the bottom of the pot. Simmer, uncovered, until the broth thickens, about 25 minutes.

6 Add the shrimp and cook just until cooked through, about 2 minutes more. Remove the pot from the heat and stir in the filé powder (if using).

7 To serve, spoon some steamed rice into each serving bowl and top with the gumbo. Garnish with the scallions and serve hot.

Mexican Pork and Sweet Potato Stew

SERVES 6 · PREP: 10 MINUTES · COOK: 1 HOUR & 15 MINUTES

ONE POT

2 tablespoons olive oil

1 onion, diced

2 garlic cloves, minced

1½ pounds boneless pork shoulder, trimmed and cut into 1½-inch cubes

6 ounces Mexican chorizo, casing removed

1 large, orange-fleshed sweet potato, peeled and diced

1 (28-ounce) can diced tomatoes, with juice

2 canned chipotle chiles in adobo sauce, minced, plus 1 tablespoon of the sauce

1 tablespoon Worcestershire sauce

1 teaspoon crumbled dried oregano

½ teaspoon kosher salt

I learned early on in my relationship with my husband that big pots of stewed pork with Mexican flavors were the way to his heart. This rich stew combines meaty pork shoulder, spicy Mexican chorizo, and sweet potatoes with layers of Mexican flavors, including smoky chipotle chiles and oregano. Serve it with warm corn tortillas, diced avocado, and crumbled queso fresco or feta cheese. You can find chipotles in adobo sauce in the international foods aisle of many supermarkets or in Mexican markets, or substitute 1 or 2 seeded and minced jalapeños and ½ teaspoon of ground chipotle powder.

1 In the Dutch oven, heat the oil over medium-high heat. Add the onion and garlic and cook, stirring frequently, until softened, about 5 minutes. Remove the onions and garlic from the pot using a slotted spoon. Add the pork and chorizo and cook, turning the pork occasionally until it is browned on all sides, about 8 minutes. Drain any excess fat from the pot.

2 Stir in the sweet potato, tomatoes, chipotles, chipotle sauce, Worcestershire, oregano, and salt and stir to mix thoroughly. Bring to a boil, reduce the heat, cover, and let simmer for 50 to 60 minutes, until the pork is very tender. Serve hot.

Beef Bourguignon

SERVES 8 TO 10 · PREP: 15 MINUTES · COOK: 2 HOURS & 30 MINUTES

6 ounces bacon, diced

4 pounds chuck roast, cut into 2-inch pieces

1½ teaspoons kosher salt, plus additional as needed

1 teaspoon freshly ground black pepper, plus additional as needed

3 tablespoons all-purpose flour

1 tablespoon olive oil

1 onion, sliced

2 large carrots, peeled and cut into 1-inch pieces

¼ cup tomato paste

3 cups dry red wine

2 cups beef broth

2 bay leaves

1 tablespoon chopped fresh thyme

1 pound frozen pearl onions

2 tablespoons unsalted butter

1 pound button or cremini mushrooms, quartered

½ cup chopped flat-leaf parsley, for garnish

Braised for hours in red wine, beef becomes extremely tender and succulent. This stew is loaded with carrots, mushrooms, and pearl onions in a rich sauce, flavored with bacon and herbs.

1 Preheat the oven to 450°F.

2 In the Dutch oven, cook the bacon over medium-high heat, stirring frequently, until crisp, about 5 minutes. Remove with a slotted spoon to a paper towel–lined plate.

3 Pat the meat dry with paper towels. In a large bowl, sprinkle the meat with salt and pepper, then toss it with the flour to coat.

4 Add the oil and meat to the Dutch oven and brown the meat on all sides (brown the meat in batches to avoid crowding the pot), until well browned, about 10 minutes total. Transfer the meat to a bowl and set aside.

5 Add the onion and carrots to the Dutch oven, season with additional salt and pepper, and cook, stirring, until the onions begin to brown, about 5 minutes. Stir in the tomato paste, wine, broth, bay leaves, and thyme and bring to a boil. Stir in the pearl onions. Return the meat, along with any juices, and the bacon back to the pot, cover, and transfer to the oven. Cook for 2 hours.

6 While the stew is in the oven, melt the butter in a skillet over medium-high heat. Add the mushrooms and sauté until they are softened and beginning to brown, about 10 minutes.

7 Remove the stew from the oven and stir in the sautéed mushrooms. Serve hot, garnished with the parsley.

Beef Chili with Butternut Squash

SERVES 6 • PREP: 15 MINUTES • COOK: 2 HOURS & 30 MINUTES

ONE POT

2 tablespoons vegetable oil, divided

2½ pounds boneless chuck roast, trimmed and cut into ½-inch cubes

¾ teaspoon kosher salt

¼ teaspoon freshly ground black pepper

1 large onion, diced

1 green bell pepper, diced

2 tablespoons tomato paste

1 tablespoon minced fresh garlic

1 to 2 jalapeño chiles, diced

⅔ cup dry red wine

1½ teaspoons ground ancho chile powder

1 teaspoon dried oregano

A big pot of chili is always welcome, whether you're watching a game with friends or resting up at home after an active weekend. This beef chili is sweetened with butternut squash, which adds color, flavor, and texture to the meaty stew.

1 In the Dutch oven, heat 1 tablespoon of oil over medium-high heat. Season the beef with the salt and pepper and brown it on all sides (brown the meat in batches to avoid crowding the pot), about 10 to 12 minutes total. Transfer the browned beef to a bowl and set aside.

2 Add the remaining 1 tablespoon of oil to the Dutch oven. Add the onion and bell pepper and cook, stirring frequently, until softened, about 5 minutes.

3 Stir in the tomato paste, garlic, and jalapeño and cook, stirring, for another 2 minutes. Add the wine and bring the liquid to a boil, stirring and scraping up any browned bits from the bottom of the pot. Cook until most of the liquid has evaporated, about 2 minutes more.

½ teaspoon cayenne pepper

¼ teaspoon ground coriander

¼ teaspoon ground cumin

⅛ teaspoon cinnamon

1 (28-ounce) can diced tomatoes

3 cups peeled and cubed (½-inch) butternut squash

2 carrots, peeled and chopped

1 (15-ounce) can pinto beans, drained and rinsed

¼ cup chopped cilantro, for garnish

4 Stir in the ancho chile powder, oregano, cayenne, coriander, cumin, cinnamon, and tomatoes. Bring to a boil over medium-high heat, then cover and reduce the heat to medium. Simmer for 1 hour.

5 Stir in the squash, carrots, and beans and continue to simmer, uncovered, until the beef and vegetables are tender and the sauce has thickened, about 1 hour more.

6 Garnish with cilantro and serve.

Did You Know? Most of the heat in hot chile peppers comes from the seeds and ribs. If you like a milder chili, remove the seeds and ribs from the jalapeño before dicing it and adding it to the pot. For a hearty kick, leave them in.

One-Pot Pasta
Puttanesca (page 95)

Chapter Five

Meatless Mains

Butternut Squash Lasagna with Spinach Béchamel

SERVES 4 • PREP: 20 MINUTES, PLUS 10 MINUTES TO REST LASAGNA • COOK: 1 HOUR & 15 MINUTES

1 tablespoon olive oil

3 garlic cloves, minced

1 onion, diced

Kosher salt

Freshly ground
black pepper

4 cups milk, divided

¼ cup cornstarch

2 (5-ounce) packages fresh
baby spinach

½ cup chopped flat-leaf
parsley, plus additional
for garnish

¼ teaspoon freshly
grated nutmeg

12 lasagna noodles, cooked
according to package
directions

1 medium butternut squash
(about 2½ pounds),
peeled, halved length-
wise, seeded, and sliced
¼-inch thick

2 cups shredded mozzarella
cheese, divided

½ cup freshly grated
Parmesan cheese

A Dutch oven is a perfect vessel for creating a deep-dish lasagna with delightfully crispy edges. This one uses a short-cut béchamel sauce laced with baby spinach and layered with sweet, tender butternut squash, noodles, and cheese.

1 Preheat the oven to 400°F.

2 In the Dutch oven, heat the oil over medium-high heat. Add the garlic and onion and season with salt and pepper. Cook, stirring occasionally, until softened and beginning to brown, about 10 minutes.

3 While the onions are browning, in a small bowl, whisk together ½ cup of milk and the cornstarch.

4 In a large saucepan, heat the remaining 3½ cups of milk until it bubbles.

5 Stir in the cornstarch mixture and bring to a boil. Cook, stirring constantly, until the mixture becomes thick, about 5 minutes.

6 Add the sautéed onions and garlic to the milk mixture along with the spinach, ½ cup of parsley, and the nutmeg. Cook, stirring, just until the spinach wilts, 1 to 2 minutes. Taste and adjust the seasoning if needed and remove from the heat.

7 Spread about ¾ cup of sauce mixture over the bottom of the Dutch oven. Arrange three noodles, slightly overlapping, to cover the bottom of the pot, cutting the noodles as needed. Lay one-third of the squash slices over the noodles, sprinkle with ½ cup of mozzarella cheese, and top with ¾ cup of sauce. Repeat with two more layers of noodles, squash slices, mozzarella cheese, and sauce. Finish with a layer of noodles, the remaining sauce, the remaining mozzarella cheese, and the Parmesan cheese.

8 Cover and bake for 40 minutes. Remove the lid of the pot and continue to bake for another 15 minutes, until the squash is tender and the cheese is melted and lightly browned. Let rest for at least 10 minutes before serving. Serve hot, garnished with parsley.

Essential Technique: A butternut squash can be tough to cut into when raw. To soften it up and make it easy to cut, microwave it on High for about 5 minutes.

Shakshuka with Eggplant and Feta

SERVES 4 • PREP: 15 MINUTES • COOK: 30 MINUTES

ONE POT

WEEKNIGHT WIN

1 large eggplant, cut
    into cubes

1 tablespoon kosher salt,
    plus additional for
    seasoning

3 garlic cloves, minced

⅓ cup chopped flat-leaf
    parsley, plus additional
    for garnish (optional)

⅓ cup chopped cilantro,
    plus additional for
    garnish (optional)

1 tablespoon paprika

1 teaspoon ground cumin

1 hot red chile, minced

2 tablespoons olive oil

½ onion, diced

4 tomatoes, roughly
    chopped, or
    1 (14.5-ounce) can
    diced tomatoes,
    drained

1 (14.5-ounce) tomato purée

Juice of ½ lemon

Freshly ground
    black pepper

4 large eggs

2 ounces crumbled
    feta cheese

A Tunisian friend introduced me to a version of this simple dish, which is essentially eggs poached in a spiced tomato sauce. The eggplant is not traditional, but it adds a velvety texture and richness. Shaksuka is often served for breakfast in Tunisia, but it is also perfectly acceptable as a satisfying breakfast-for-dinner meal.

1 Place the eggplant in a strainer or colander set over a bowl or sink and toss it with 1 tablespoon of salt. Let sit for about 10 minutes.

2 In a small bowl, stir together the garlic, ⅓ cup of parsley, ⅓ cup of cilantro, the paprika, the cumin, and the chile.

3 Rinse the eggplant and squeeze it gently to release excess moisture.

4 In the Dutch oven, heat the oil over medium-high heat. Add the onion and cook, stirring frequently, until softened, about 5 minutes.

5 Add the eggplant and cook, stirring, until the eggplant begins to brown, about 5 minutes more.

6 Stir in the tomatoes, tomato purée, lemon juice, and the garlic and spice mixture. Season with salt and pepper and bring to a simmer. Cook, uncovered, for 15 minutes, until the sauce thickens.

7 Using a wooden spoon, form four divots in the surface of the vegetable mixture. Crack an egg into each divot. Sprinkle the feta cheese over the top, cover, and cook, until the egg whites are set and the yolks are still a bit runny, about 6 minutes.

8 To serve, scoop a portion of the vegetable mixture, along with one of the eggs, into each of four serving bowls. Serve hot, garnished with additional parsley and/or cilantro (if using).

Make It a Meal: All you need to make this comforting dish into a meal is a loaf of crusty bread, which is absolutely essential for soaking up the rich, flavorful sauce.

Ratatouille

SERVES 4 • PREP: 20 MINUTES • COOK: 1 HOUR & 20 MINUTES

ONE POT

2 large eggplants, peeled
and cut into cubes

1 tablespoon kosher salt,
plus additional
for seasoning

5 teaspoons olive oil,
divided

2 onions, diced

2 red or green bell peppers,
seeded and cut
into strips

6 to 8 medium zucchini,
cut into cubes

4 garlic cloves, minced

4 large tomatoes, diced

1 bay leaf

4 sprigs fresh thyme

1 tablespoon red wine
vinegar

Originating in southern France, this classic dish is loaded with fresh summer vegetables—tomatoes, eggplant, summer squashes—plus lots of flavorful onions, garlic, and fresh herbs. This recipe follows the traditional approach of sautéing each ingredient separately at first, and then layering them together to be baked into a cohesive casserole. Serve it with plenty of crusty bread.

1 Place the eggplant cubes in a strainer or colander set over a bowl or sink and toss with 1 tablespoon of salt. Let sit for about 15 minutes.

2 Meanwhile, in the Dutch oven, heat 1 teaspoon of oil over medium-high heat. Add the onions, season with salt, and cook, stirring frequently, until the onions have softened and are beginning to brown, about 8 minutes.

3 Stir in the peppers and cook, stirring occasionally, about 5 minutes more. Transfer the onions and peppers to a large bowl and set aside.

4 Add another 1 teaspoon of oil to the pot along with the zucchini and a pinch of salt. Cook, stirring occasionally, until the zucchini begin to brown, about 5 minutes. Add the zucchini to the bowl with the onions and peppers. **>>**

5 Rinse the eggplant and squeeze gently to release excess moisture. Add 2 teaspoons of oil to the pot and cook the eggplant, stirring occasionally, until it has softened, about 10 minutes. Add the eggplant to the bowl of cooked vegetables.

6 Preheat the oven to 400°F.

7 In the Dutch oven, heat the remaining 1 teaspoon of olive oil, add the garlic, and cook, stirring, for 1 minute. Stir in the tomatoes, bay leaf, and thyme and bring to a simmer. Cook, stirring and scraping up any browned bits from the bottom of the pot, about 3 minutes. Return all the vegetables to the pot and stir to combine. Reduce the heat to low and simmer. Transfer the pot to the oven and bake, uncovered, until bubbling, about 15 to 20 minutes. Stir in the vinegar and taste and adjust seasoning if necessary. Remove and discard the bay leaf and thyme sprigs. Serve hot.

Essential Technique: Salting the eggplant before cooking it helps to draw out excess liquid, which improves the texture once it's cooked and reduces bitterness.

One-Pot Pasta Puttanesca

SERVES 4 • PREP: 10 MINUTES • COOK: 15 MINUTES

¼ cup olive oil

6 garlic cloves, minced

4 anchovy fillets or
    2 teaspoons white miso

1½ teaspoons dried
    oregano

¾ teaspoon red
    pepper flakes

24 Kalamata olives, pitted
    and chopped

3 tablespoons capers

4 cups vegetable broth
    or water

12 ounces dried penne

3 pints cherry or grape
    tomatoes, halved

2 tablespoons tomato paste

¼ cup chopped fresh basil

¼ cup chopped
    flat-leaf parsley

⅛ teaspoon kosher salt

Freshly ground
    black pepper

Parmesan cheese, for
    serving (optional)

This one-pot pasta dish combines sweet, tangy tomatoes with capers, and olives for a simple yet deliciously rustic meal. It traditionally includes salty, briny anchovies for deep umami flavor, but you can substitute white miso—which you can find in many supermarkets, health-food stores, or Asian markets—if you wish to keep the recipe vegetarian.

1 In the Dutch oven, heat the oil over medium heat. Add the garlic, anchovies or miso paste, oregano, and red pepper flakes and cook, stirring, for 2 minutes.

2 Stir in the olives and capers. Add the broth along with the dried pasta and bring to a boil. Cook, uncovered, stirring occasionally, for 10 minutes.

3 Stir in the tomatoes and tomato paste and continue to cook until the pasta is tender, 2 to 3 minutes more.

4 Remove the pot from the heat and stir in the basil, parsley, and salt. Serve hot, seasoned with black pepper, and served with Parmesan cheese (if using).

Oven-Baked Mac & Cheese with Crispy Bread Crumbs

SERVES 6 • PREP: 15 MINUTES, PLUS 10 MINUTES TO REST MAC & CHEESE • COOK: 40 MINUTES

FOR THE TOPPING

2 tablespoons
   unsalted butter

2 tablespoons olive oil

2 cups panko bread crumbs

2 garlic cloves, minced

2 ounces (about ½ cup)
   grated Parmesan cheese

½ teaspoon kosher salt

This simple, straightforward mac and cheese is the kind of dish you dream about. It's tangy, cheesy, and creamy and has a little kick from mustard powder (and cayenne, if you use it), yet it's basic enough to please even super picky eaters (read: kids!). The crunchy, garlicky topping is what puts it over the top for me.

TO MAKE THE TOPPING

1 In the Dutch oven, heat the butter with the oil over medium-high heat, cooking until the butter foams and then the foam subsides.

2 Stir in the bread crumbs and garlic and cook, stirring constantly, until the bread crumbs are golden brown, about 5 minutes. Transfer the mixture to a bowl and stir in the Parmesan cheese and salt.

TO MAKE THE MAC & CHEESE

1 Preheat the oven to 400°F.

2 In the Dutch oven, melt the butter over medium-low heat. While whisking, sprinkle the flour over the butter. Cook, continuing to whisk constantly, until the mixture turns golden brown, about 5 minutes.

FOR THE MAC & CHEESE

¼ cup unsalted butter

3 tablespoons
all-purpose flour

2 cups whole milk

6 tablespoons heavy cream

2 teaspoons
mustard powder

1 teaspoon kosher salt

½ teaspoon paprika
(optional)

¼ teaspoon cayenne
pepper (optional)

14 ounces (about 5½ cups)
extra-sharp
Cheddar cheese

2 ounces (about ½ cup)
grated Parmesan cheese

4 cups dried elbow macaroni
noodles, cooked al dente
(remove from the heat
and drain 2 or 3 minutes
before the cooking time
listed on the package)

3 Slowly add the milk and cream, still whisking constantly, until they are incorporated. Still whisking constantly, increase the heat to medium-high and bring the mixture just to a boil. Reduce the heat to medium-low and simmer, stirring occasionally, until the sauce is thick enough to coat the back of a spoon, about 3 minutes more.

4 Stir in the mustard powder, salt, paprika (if using), and cayenne (if using). Add the Cheddar and Parmesan cheeses, 1 to 2 cups at a time, whisking after each addition until the cheese melts completely. Remove the pot from the heat.

5 Add the cooked and drained pasta to the cheese sauce and stir until it is well coated. Spread the mixture into an even layer and sprinkle the bread crumb topping evenly over the top.

6 Bake, uncovered, for about 20 minutes, until the sauce is bubbling and the topping is golden brown. Let it rest about 10 minutes before serving. Serve hot.

Make It a Meal: I serve this rich pasta dish with humble steamed broccoli. The broccoli is fresh, green, and light enough to cut some of the richness of the pasta. Plus, my kid likes it.

Smoked Tofu and Corn Chili

SERVES 4 • PREP: 10 MINUTES • COOK: 40 MINUTES

ONE POT

2 tablespoons olive oil

1 large onion, diced

4 garlic cloves, minced

2 large poblano chiles, seeded and finely diced

1 large red bell pepper, seeded and chopped

1 jalapeño chile, seeded and minced

¼ teaspoon chili powder

1 teaspoon ground cumin

1 (28-ounce) can crushed tomatoes

1 cup canned tomato sauce

½ teaspoon dried oregano

1 teaspoon kosher salt

1 pound smoked tofu, diced

1 (19-ounce) can pinto beans, drained and rinsed

1½ cups fresh or frozen corn kernels

½ cup cilantro, for garnish

This hearty vegetarian chili gets its smoky flavor from smoked tofu, which you can buy in the refrigerator section of many supermarkets and most health food stores, or you can substitute regular baked tofu. This is one of those dishes that get better as they sit, so make it a day ahead if you can. Serve a pan of cornbread alongside.

1 In the Dutch oven, heat the oil over medium heat. Add the onions, garlic, chiles, bell pepper, and jalapeño and cook, stirring occasionally, until softened, about 8 minutes.

2 Stir in the chili powder and cumin and cook for about 2 minutes more.

3 Add the tomatoes, tomato sauce, oregano, and salt and bring to a simmer. Reduce the heat to maintain a gentle simmer and cook, stirring occasionally, for about 15 minutes.

4 Add the tofu and beans and continue to simmer for another 10 minutes or so, until the flavors meld.

5 Stir in the corn and let the chili simmer for another 3 minutes or so, until heated through.

6 Serve hot, garnished with cilantro.

Chickpea and Cauliflower Tikka Masala

SERVES 4 • PREP: 10 MINUTES • COOK: 25 MINUTES

ONE POT

WEEKNIGHT WIN

2 tablespoons olive oil

1 onion, diced

4 garlic cloves, minced

Pinch of kosher salt

1 tablespoon garam masala

1 (2-inch) piece of fresh ginger, grated

1 fresh jalapeño chile, stemmed, seeded, and minced

1 (15-ounce) can chickpeas, drained and rinsed

2 (14.5-ounce) cans diced tomatoes

1 small head cauliflower, cut into florets

1 cup of full-fat coconut milk

¼ cup chopped cilantro, plus additional for garnish

This easy vegan curry gets the majority of its flavor, and its name, from the Indian spice mixture garam masala. It's a combination that almost always includes cumin, coriander, cinnamon, black pepper, and cardamom, with other spices added to some versions. You can usually find it in the supermarket's spice aisle, but if not, it's readily available online. Serve this stew over steamed rice or with naan or another type of flatbread for scooping up the juicy goodness.

1 In the Dutch oven, heat the oil over medium heat. Add the onion, garlic, and salt and cook, stirring frequently, until the onion is softened and beginning to brown, about 5 minutes. Stir in the garam masala, ginger, and jalapeño and cook, stirring, for 1 minute more.

2 Add the chickpeas, tomatoes, and cauliflower. Bring to a boil and then reduce the heat to medium-low. Simmer until the cauliflower is tender, about 15 minutes.

3 Stir in the coconut milk and simmer for an additional 5 minutes.

4 Remove the pot from the heat and stir in the cilantro. Serve hot, garnished with additional cilantro.

Vegetarian Cassoulet with Roasted Butternut Squash and Caramelized Onions

SERVES 4 • PREP: 10 MINUTES • COOK: 1 HOUR & 20 MINUTES

ONE POT

5 tablespoons olive oil, divided

6 garlic cloves, unpeeled

2 medium onions, halved and thickly sliced

1 teaspoon kosher salt, plus additional for seasoning

2 pounds cubed butternut squash

2 tablespoons red wine vinegar

2 (15-ounce) cans cannellini beans or other white beans, drained and rinsed

1 cup vegetable broth

1 tablespoon chopped fresh thyme

½ teaspoon freshly ground black pepper

2 bay leaves

2 cups panko bread crumbs

½ cup grated Parmesan cheese

¼ cup chopped flat-leaf parsley, for garnish

Traditional cassoulet is usually piled with rich meats like sausage and duck legs. This vegetarian version is much lighter, but just as satisfying. The sweet caramelized onions and squash add depth to the flavor, and the beans make it plenty filling. Serve it with a simple side salad for a perfect vegetarian meal on a chilly night.

1 Preheat the oven to 375°F.

2 In the Dutch oven, heat 2 tablespoons of oil over medium heat. Add the garlic and onions, season with salt, and cook, stirring frequently, until the onions are very soft and browned, about 15 minutes. Transfer the garlic and onions to a bowl.

3 In the Dutch oven, heat 2 tablespoons of the remaining oil over medium-high heat. Add the squash, beans, broth, thyme, 1 teaspoon of salt, pepper, and bay leaves.

4 In a small bowl, stir together the bread crumbs, Parmesan cheese, and remaining 1 tablespoon of olive oil. Sprinkle the bread crumb mixture evenly over the bean mixture. Cover and bake for 45 to 50 minutes, until the squash is tender.

5 Remove the lid and continue to bake, uncovered, until the topping is crisp and golden brown, about 15 minutes more.

6 Serve hot, garnished with the parsley.

Leek and Wild Mushroom Risotto with Parmesan

SERVES 4 • PREP: 10 MINUTES • COOK: 35 MINUTES

7 cups chicken broth

7 tablespoons unsalted butter, divided

1½ pounds fresh wild mushrooms (porcini, chanterelle, shiitake, hen of the woods, or a combination), sliced or halved if small

Kosher salt

Freshly ground black pepper

1 tablespoon olive oil

¾ cup finely chopped leek (white and pale green parts only)

1¼ cups Arborio rice

½ cup dry white wine

¼ cup grated Parmesan cheese, plus additional for serving (optional)

Risotto is a bit fussy to make since you have to stir it continuously while adding broth a little at a time, but it is always well received. The Dutch oven is great for cooking risotto since it retains heat so well and heats evenly so that you don't end up with any hot spots in the pot. A mixture of fresh wild mushrooms makes this simple risotto elegant, but if you can't find any, feel free to substitute cultivated button, cremini, or shiitake mushrooms.

1 In a large saucepan, bring the chicken broth to a simmer and keep warm.

2 In the Dutch oven, melt 4 tablespoons of butter over medium-high heat. Add the mushrooms, season with salt and pepper, and cook, stirring frequently, until softened and browned, about 5 minutes (you may need to cook the mushrooms in batches to avoid crowding the pot). Transfer the mushrooms to a bowl.

3 In the Dutch oven, heat the remaining 3 tablespoons of butter with the olive oil. Reduce the heat to medium-low, add the leek, season with salt, and cook, stirring frequently, until softened, about 5 minutes.

4 Increase the heat to medium, add the rice, and cook, stirring, until the rice is well coated with the butter and oil and begins to look translucent, about 3 minutes.

5 Add the wine and cook, stirring, until the liquid is fully absorbed, about 1 minute.

6 Begin adding the warm broth, ¾ cup at a time, stirring after each addition until the liquid is nearly absorbed. After about 10 minutes of adding broth ¾ cup at a time, stir in the mushrooms and then resume adding broth ¾ cup at a time and stirring until it is mostly absorbed, about 10 minutes more, until the rice is creamy and tender, but still al dente.

7 Stir in the Parmesan cheese and serve immediately, with extra Parmesan cheese for sprinkling on top (if using).

Creamy Mushroom Stroganoff with Kale

SERVES 4 • PREP: 15 MINUTES • COOK: 25 MINUTES

WEEKNIGHT WIN

½ ounce (about ½ cup) dried porcini mushrooms

2 cups boiling water

8 ounces dried egg noodles

3 tablespoons olive oil, divided

8 ounces fresh cremini mushrooms, stems trimmed and sliced ¼-inch thick

1 onion, diced

½ teaspoon paprika

2 tablespoons all-purpose flour

¾ pound kale, tough center ribs removed and leaves julienned

3 garlic cloves, minced

Kosher salt

Freshly ground black pepper

¼ cup dry white wine

2 tablespoons unsalted butter

⅓ cup sour cream

¼ cup chopped flat-leaf parsley, for garnish

This meat-free version of a classic comfort food dish delivers deep, rich umami flavor thanks to meaty mushrooms, including super-flavorful dried porcinis and their soaking liquid. Adding kale rounds out the dish, making it a suitable quick meal.

1 In a heatproof bowl, place the dried porcini and pour the boiling water over them. Soak the mushrooms for about 10 minutes. Using a slotted spoon or fork, remove the mushrooms from the water (reserve the soaking water) and chop them. Strain 1½ cups of the mushroom soaking liquid, leaving behind the gritty sediment that has settled on the bottom of the bowl, and reserve. Discard the remaining soaking liquid and sediment.

2 In a large pot, bring heavily salted water to a boil over high heat. Cook the noodles according to the package directions, reserving ⅓ cup of cooking water before draining them.

3 In the Dutch oven, heat 1 tablespoon of oil over medium-high heat. Add the cremini mushrooms and cook, stirring occasionally, until they are softened and browned, about 5 minutes. Transfer the mushrooms to a medium bowl and add the chopped porcini.

4 Reduce the heat to medium and heat the remaining 2 tablespoons of oil. Add the onion and paprika and cook, stirring frequently, until softened, about 5 minutes.

5 Sprinkle the flour over the onions and cook, stirring occasionally, for 2 minutes. Stir in the kale and garlic, season with salt and pepper, and cook, stirring, just until the kale wilts, about 1 minute.

6 Stir in the reserved cremini and porcini mushrooms, along with any juices that have accumulated in the bowl. Add the wine, bring to a boil, and cook for about 3 minutes, until most of the liquid has evaporated.

7 Reduce the heat to low, add the reserved mushroom-soaking liquid, season with salt and pepper, and cook, stirring and scraping up any browned bits from the bottom of the pot, for about 5 minutes, until the sauce thickens.

8 Add the reserved pasta cooking water to the sauce and simmer until thickened, about 2 minutes. Stir in the butter and cook until melted, about 2 minutes more.

9 Remove the pot from the heat, add the sour cream, and stir until combined.

10 To serve, mound some of the noodles in a pasta bowl, top with the sauce, and garnish with the parsley. Serve hot.

Mussels and Cod in
a Thai Lemongrass
Broth (page 108)

Chapter Six

Fish & Seafood Mains

Mussels and Cod in a Thai Lemongrass Broth

SERVES 4 · PREP: 10 MINUTES · COOK: 10 MINUTES

ONE POT

WEEKNIGHT WIN

2 tablespoons vegetable oil

½ teaspoon sesame oil

1 stalk fresh lemongrass, white part only, finely minced

1 small shallot, diced

2 scallions, green parts only, thinly sliced

1 garlic clove, minced

1-inch piece fresh ginger, peeled and minced

½ teaspoon red pepper flakes

1 cup bottled clam juice

1 cup unsweetened coconut milk

Finely grated zest of 1 lime

1½ teaspoons rice vinegar

1½ teaspoons sugar

¼ teaspoon kosher salt

1½ pounds fresh mussels

¾ pound cod fillets, cut into 2-inch pieces

½ cup chopped cilantro

½ cup flat-leaf parsley, for garnish

Easy to cook, inexpensive, and extremely tasty, mussels may be the most overlooked shellfish. Here they are steamed in a coconut milk broth that infuses them with the spicy sweet flavors of lemongrass, garlic, ginger, and chile. Be sure to serve lots of crusty bread for dunking into the broth, and give everyone a spoon, too, because they'll want to slurp up every last drop.

1 In the Dutch oven, heat the vegetable oil and sesame oil over medium-high heat. When the oil begins to shimmer, add the lemongrass, shallot, scallions, garlic, ginger, and red pepper flakes and cook, stirring, just until fragrant, about 15 seconds.

2 Add the clam juice, coconut milk, lime zest, vinegar, sugar, and salt and bring to a boil. Add the mussels and cod and stir to coat. Cover the pot and cook for about 5 minutes, until most of the mussels open (discard any mussels that don't open) and the cod is opaque and cooked through.

3 Remove the cover and stir in the cilantro. Serve immediately, garnished with parsley.

Essential Technique: Before cooking live mussels, rinse them under cold water and pull off any stringy beards. If any of the mussels are open, tap them with a spoon. If the shell closes up, you can be assured that the mussel is still alive and safe for cooking. If it doesn't close up, toss it.

Dutch Oven Clam Bake

SERVES 4 • PREP: 10 MINUTES • COOK: 40 MINUTES

ONE POT

1 tablespoon olive oil

1 onion, diced

1 leek (white part only), diced

1 pound small red potatoes

1¾ teaspoons kosher salt, divided

½ teaspoon freshly ground black pepper

8 ounces smoked or cured sausage (such as Spanish chorizo, linguica, kielbasa, or andouille), sliced

2 ears of corn, halved

3 pounds small clams, such as manilas or littlenecks

1 cup dry white wine

1 teaspoon chili powder

1 teaspoon grated lemon zest

1 teaspoon fresh thyme leaves

½ cup melted butter, for dipping

This simple one-pot clam bake is perfect for serving outside on a summer day. Cold beer, crusty bread for dunking in the broth, and a whole lot of napkins are the only accompaniments you need. If you've got a larger Dutch oven, double the recipe, adding other shellfish like mussels, shrimp, or lobster in addition to the clams.

1 In the Dutch oven, heat the oil over medium heat. Add the onion and leek and cook, stirring, until they begin to brown, about 10 minutes.

2 Arrange the potatoes on top of the onion in a single layer and season with ¾ teaspoon of salt and the pepper. Top with a layer of sausage, and then corn, and then the clams. Add the wine, cover, and cook over medium-high heat until steam begins to escape from the pot, about 15 minutes.

3 Reduce the heat to medium and continue to cook until the clams are open and the potatoes are tender, about 15 minutes more.

4 In a small bowl, stir together the chili powder, remaining 1 teaspoon of salt, lemon zest, and thyme.

5 Scoop the clams and vegetables out of the pot with a wooden spoon and transfer them to a large serving bowl. Pour the broth over the clams and vegetables, being careful to leave behind any grit that has settled in the pot.

6 Sprinkle the spice mixture over the top and serve immediately, with melted butter for dipping.

Shrimp Creole

SERVES 4 · PREP: 15 MINUTES · COOK: 1 HOUR & 10 MINUTES

ONE POT

2 tablespoons unsalted
  butter

1 tablespoon vegetable oil

1 onion, diced

4 garlic cloves, minced

2 celery stalks, diced

1 green bell pepper, diced

1 teaspoon paprika

1 teaspoon kosher salt, plus
  additional for seasoning

1 teaspoon freshly ground
  black pepper, plus
  additional for seasoning

½ teaspoon cayenne pepper

½ teaspoon dried oregano

2 tablespoons tomato paste

1 (28-ounce) can diced
  tomatoes, drained

½ cup dry white wine

A classic shrimp dish from southern Louisiana, shrimp Creole varies in its ingredients from cook to cook, but all start with the holy trinity of Creole cooking: onions, peppers, and celery. Tomatoes turn it into a saucy mixture spiced with cayenne, thyme, oregano, bay leaves, and garlic—hallmarks of Louisiana cuisine. The sauce simmers down to a rich, thick gravy that the plump, tender shrimp are cooked in. Served over white rice, it makes a deeply satisfying meal.

1 In the Dutch oven, heat the butter and vegetable oil over medium-high heat. When the butter begins to foam, add the onion and garlic and cook, stirring occasionally, until the onion is softened and golden brown, about 5 minutes.

2 Stir in the celery, bell pepper, paprika, salt, pepper, cayenne, and oregano. Reduce the heat to medium, and cook, stirring occasionally, until the vegetables soften, about 5 minutes more.

3 Add the tomato paste and cook, stirring constantly, until its color begins to darken.

4 Add the tomatoes and a pinch of salt, and continue to cook, stirring occasionally, until the tomatoes begin to break down, about 5 minutes more.

2 cups shrimp stock
or clam juice

2 bay leaves

4 sprigs fresh thyme

2 tablespoons
all-purpose flour

1 cup water

1 tablespoon hot
pepper sauce

1 tablespoon
Worcestershire sauce

2 pounds peeled and
deveined shrimp

4 scallions, thinly sliced

2 tablespoons minced
flat-leaf parsley

Cooked white rice,
for serving

5 Add the wine and increase the heat to high. Cook, stirring and scraping up any browned bits from the bottom of the pot, until the liquid is mostly evaporated.

6 Add the shrimp stock, bay leaves, and thyme. Bring to a boil, reduce the heat, and simmer, uncovered, for 40 to 45 minutes.

7 In a small bowl, whisk together the flour and water until well combined. Add the flour mixture to the Dutch oven and cook, stirring to mix well, until the sauce thickens, 4 to 6 minutes more.

8 Stir in the hot sauce, Worcestershire, and shrimp. Reduce the heat and simmer until the shrimp are opaque, 4 to 6 minutes. Remove the bay leaves and thyme sprigs and discard them.

9 Stir in the scallions and parsley and serve hot, spooned over rice.

Perfect Pairing: A crisp lager-style beer would be great to counteract the heat of this dish. Likewise a crisp Riesling with a hint of sweetness or a citrusy Sauvignon Blanc would pair nicely with the sweet shrimp and spicy sauce.

Alentejo-Style Clam and Pork Stew

SERVES 6 • PREP: 10 MINUTES • COOK: 1 HOUR & 15 MINUTES

ONE POT

2 pounds boneless pork shoulder, cut into 1-inch cubes

1 teaspoon kosher salt

½ teaspoon freshly ground black pepper

½ cup all-purpose flour

3 tablespoons olive oil

2 onions, diced

4 garlic cloves, minced

1 large green bell pepper, seeded and diced

8 ounces Portuguese linguica, halved lengthwise and sliced

2 tablespoons paprika

1 bay leaf

1 tablespoon minced fresh thyme

1 cup dry white wine

1 cup chicken broth

1 (14.5-ounce) can diced tomatoes

2 pounds small clams

2 tablespoons chopped cilantro

2 tablespoons chopped flat-leaf parsley, plus additional for garnish

This is a classic dish from the Alentejo region of Portugal, which produces some of the world's best pork. The meaty pork is simmered until very tender and then clams are steamed in the flavorful broth. This version includes Portuguese linguica sausage as well, or you can substitute Spanish chorizo.

1 Season the pork all over with the salt and pepper and then dredge in the flour.

2 In the Dutch oven, heat the oil over medium-high heat. Add the pork and cook (in batches if necessary to avoid crowding the pot), turning occasionally, until browned on all sides, about 8 minutes. Transfer the browned meat to a plate.

3 Add the onions, garlic, bell pepper, and sausage to the pot and cook, stirring frequently, until the onions have softened, about 5 minutes. Stir in the paprika, bay leaf, and thyme and then add the wine and cook, stirring, for about 2 minutes.

4 Add the broth and tomatoes and bring to a boil.

5 Return the pork to the pot, along with any juices that have accumulated, and reduce the heat to medium-low. Cover and simmer until the meat is very tender, about 50 minutes.

6 Add the clams, cilantro, and parsley, cover, and cook for about 5 minutes more, until most of the clams have opened (discard any clams that don't open). Taste and adjust seasoning as needed, and remove and discard the bay leaf. Serve immediately, garnished with parsley.

South Indian–Style Shrimp Curry with Toasted Spices

SERVES 4 • PREP: 20 MINUTES • COOK: 15 MINUTES

1 teaspoon coriander seeds

1 teaspoon cumin seeds

1 teaspoon black
  peppercorns

½ teaspoon cloves

¼ teaspoon mustard seeds

3 cardamom pods

½ teaspoon ground ginger

½ teaspoon ground
  cinnamon

¼ teaspoon ground turmeric

2 tablespoons vegetable oil

6 serrano chiles, seeded
  and sliced into strips

4 garlic cloves, minced

Using a customized blend of whole, toasted spices makes this curry taste wholly authentic. South India produces some of the most flavorful seafood dishes in the world, thanks to a bounty of fresh fish and shellfish and a vast pantry of fresh and dried spices and herbs. In keeping with South Indian cuisine, this curry is quite spicy. If you prefer a milder dish, cut down on the number of chiles.

1 Heat the Dutch oven over medium heat. Add the coriander seeds, cumin seeds, peppercorns, cloves, mustard seeds, and cardamom pods. Toast the spices, shaking the pan frequently, until they become fragrant, about 1 minute. Transfer the toasted spices to a mortar, spice mill, or coffee grinder, removing the cardamom seeds from their pods and discarding the pods. Add the ground ginger, cinnamon, and turmeric to the spices and grind to a fine powder.

2 In the Dutch oven, heat the oil over medium heat. Add the chiles, garlic, ginger, and onion, and cook, stirring frequently, until the onion and chiles are softened, about 5 minutes.

1 tablespoon peeled and
 minced fresh ginger

1 onion, diced

1 teaspoon kosher salt

1 (14.5-ounce) can
 coconut milk

1 cup chicken broth or
 water, plus additional
 if needed

2 pounds shrimp, peeled
 and deveined

½ cup chopped tomatoes

2 bay leaves

Cooked white rice,
 for serving

¼ cup minced cilantro

3 Reduce the heat to medium and add the ground spice powder along with the salt, coconut milk, and broth. Bring to a simmer. If the sauce becomes too thick, add a bit more broth or water.

4 Add the shrimp and cook, stirring, until the shrimp just turn opaque, 3 to 4 minutes.

5 Stir in the tomatoes and bay leaves and cook for about 2 minutes more to heat through. Discard the bay leaves, and taste and adjust the seasoning if needed.

6 Serve immediately, spooned over cooked rice and garnished with cilantro.

Did You Know? Whole spice seeds, like cumin and fennel, retain more of their essential oils, and hence their flavor and aroma, than ground spices. By toasting whole spices and grinding them yourself, you capture all of those intense flavors and aromas in your dish, giving it far more flavor than if you used a powdered spice blend.

One-Pot Linguine with Clams in Garlic and Wine

SERVES 4 • PREP: 5 MINUTES • COOK: 20 MINUTES

ONE POT

WEEKNIGHT WIN

2 tablespoons olive oil

1 red onion, thinly sliced

Kosher salt

3 garlic cloves, minced

Pinch of crushed red pepper

1½ cups dry white wine

1 cup clam juice or chicken broth

12 ounces dried linguini

½ cup chopped flat-leaf parsley, divided

4 pounds small clams, such as littlenecks or manilas, scrubbed

Zest and juice of 1 lemon

Freshly ground black pepper

Seasonal Swap: In the summertime, brighten up this dish with a couple of pints of halved sungold or cherry tomatoes fresh from the garden or farmers' market. Add the tomatoes at the same time as the clams.

Linguine with clams is one of the quickest and most satisfying weeknight meals in my repertoire. It's especially easy when the pasta and sauce are cooked together in a single pot. Aside from the clams, most of the ingredients are pantry staples that you're likely to already have on hand, and the dish takes less than half an hour to get on the table. Add a simple salad and some garlic bread, and you're in weeknight-dinner heaven.

1 In the Dutch oven, heat the oil over medium-high heat. Add the onion and season with a pinch of salt. Cook, stirring frequently, until the onion begins to soften, about 3 minutes.

2 Add the garlic and crushed red pepper and cook for 30 seconds more. Stir in the wine and clam juice and bring to a boil.

3 Stir in the linguini (you can break the noodles in half before adding them to the pot or press them into the sauce as they soften until they are completely submerged). Cook at a vigorous boil for 5 minutes. Stir in ¼ cup of parsley and the clams. Cover and cook for 6 to 8 minutes, until the pasta is tender and most of the clams have opened (discard any that don't open after 8 minutes).

4 Remove from the heat, stir in the lemon zest and juice, black pepper, and the remaining ¼ cup of parsley. Serve hot.

Salmon Poached in Olive Oil

SERVES 4 • PREP: 10 MINUTES • COOK: 15 MINUTES

ONE POT

WEEKNIGHT WIN

2 sprigs fresh sage, crushed in your hands

4 (1-inch) pieces lemon peel (no bitter white pith)

2 garlic cloves, smashed

4 cups olive oil (or enough to cover the fish)

4 (6-ounce) salmon fillets, skin on

¾ teaspoon kosher salt

Freshly grated lemon zest, for garnish

Freshly squeezed lemon juice, for garnish

Flaky finishing salt, for garnish

Essential Technique: Use a vegetable peeler to shave off the yellow peel of the lemon, leaving behind any of the bitter white pith.

Poaching fish in olive oil is a simple technique that yields flaky, flavorful meat. The fish is submerged in a bath of warm olive oil flavored with herbs and cooked slowly at low temperature. When it emerges, it is incredibly tender with a silky texture, and the clean, distinct flavor of the fish shines through.

1 In the Dutch oven, combine the sage, lemon peel, garlic, and oil and heat over medium heat until the oil registers 180°F on a deep-fry thermometer. Reduce the heat to medium-low and continue to monitor the temperature to keep it around 180°F.

2 Season the fish with the salt and then add it to the Dutch oven. If the temperature of the oil drops, increase the heat a bit to bring the oil temperature back up to 180°F. Once the oil is back up to temperature, reduce the heat to low.

3 Cook for 13 to 15 minutes, until the fish is opaque and flakes apart easily when tested with a fork. Transfer the fish to a paper towel–lined plate.

4 Just before serving, sprinkle each fillet with a little lemon juice and zest, plus a little flaky salt, for garnish, and serve immediately.

Beer-Battered Fried Fish with Seasame-Soy Dipping Sauce

SERVES 4 • PREP: 10 MINUTES • COOK: 30 MINUTES

Vegetable or peanut oil, for frying

1 (12-ounce) can beer, preferably a lager

2 cups all-purpose flour, divided

2 tablespoons sesame seeds

½ teaspoon kosher salt, plus additional for seasoning

1½ pound cod fillet, cut diagonally into 1-inch-wide by 5- or 6-inch-long strips

Freshly ground black pepper

½ cup low-sodium soy sauce

¼ cup rice wine vinegar

2 tablespoons finely grated ginger

2 teaspoons sugar

1 teaspoon sesame oil

Malt vinegar, for serving

Fish and chips is a simple meal, and by making it in a Dutch oven, you can avoid most of the mess associated with deep-frying.

1 Fill the Dutch oven about half full with oil, and heat over medium-high heat until the oil registers 375°F on a deep-fry thermometer.

2 In a large bowl, whisk together the beer, 1½ cups of flour, and the sesame seeds until well combined. Stir in ½ teaspoon of salt. Place the remaining ½ cup of flour in a wide, flat bowl.

3 Pat the fish dry with paper towels and season on both sides with salt and pepper. Dunk each piece of fish in the beer batter, dredge it in the bowl of flour, and lower it gently into the hot oil. Cook several pieces of fish at a time, but be careful not to crowd the pot. Turn the fish pieces frequently as they cook, until they turn deep golden brown, about 5 minutes. Use a slotted spoon to transfer the cooked fish to a baking sheet lined with paper towels, and season with salt.

4 To make the dipping sauce, combine the soy sauce, vinegar, ginger, sugar, and sesame oil and mix well.

5 Serve hot with the dipping sauce on the side.

Essential Technique: Don't toss out your frying oil, because you can reuse it. Let it come to room temperature once you are done cooking, and then strain it through a fine-meshed sieve, or one lined with cheesecloth, into a jar.

Halibut Poached in Tomato Sauce with Chorizo

SERVES 4 • PREP: 5 MINUTES • COOK: 20 MINUTES

1½ teaspoons olive oil

6 ounces Spanish chorizo, diced

1 onion, diced

1 garlic clove, minced

1 (14.5-ounce) can diced tomatoes

1 teaspoon light brown sugar

2 teaspoons fresh thyme leaves

1 tablespoon soy sauce

4 (6-ounce) halibut fillets

¼ cup chopped flat-leaf parsley, for garnish

Slightly spicy chorizo adds depth to a simple garlicky tomato sauce, which is used as a medium to poach the fish. It's a quick, healthy, and very flavorful meal. Serve it with mashed or roasted potatoes and some sautéed greens for a perfect weeknight meal.

1 In the Dutch oven, heat the oil over medium-high heat. Add the chorizo, onion, and garlic and cook, stirring frequently, until the sausage is browned and the onion is softened, about 6 minutes.

2 Add the tomatoes, brown sugar, thyme, and soy sauce, stir to mix well, and then bring to a boil. Reduce the heat to medium and let the sauce simmer for 5 minutes.

3 Gently slide the fish fillets into the sauce, submerging them if possible. Cover and cook until the fish flakes easily when tested with a fork, about 10 minutes.

4 Serve hot, garnished with parsley.

Roasted Cod with Potatoes and Olives

SERVES 4 • PREP: 5 MINUTES • COOK: 40 MINUTES

ONE POT

WEEKNIGHT WIN

3 tablespoons olive oil

1 onion, halved and sliced

2 boiling potatoes,
   peeled and cut into
   ¼-inch-thick slices

1 garlic clove, minced

½ cup Kalamata or
   black olives cured
   in brine, pitted

4 cod fillets, about
   6 ounces each

Kosher salt

Freshly ground
   black pepper

2 tablespoons chopped flat-
   leaf parsley, for garnish

This simple yet elegant one-pot meal leverages the classic flavors and techniques of Mediterranean cooking. A meaty fish is combined with potatoes, olives, garlic, and onion—all ubiquitous ingredients in Mediterranean cuisine—and the result is simple but at the same time delightfully layered with the flavors of the region.

1 Preheat the oven to 450°F.

2 In the Dutch oven, heat the oil over medium heat. Add the onion and cook, stirring occasionally, until the slices soften, about 5 minutes.

3 Add the potatoes and garlic and cook, turning the potatoes occasionally, until they are pale golden, about 10 minutes.

4 Remove from the heat, stir in the olives, and then push the vegetable mixture to the sides creating an empty space in the bottom of the pot.

5 Season the fillets generously on both sides with salt and pepper and place them in the Dutch oven. Push the vegetable mixture around and over the fish. Roast, uncovered, until the fish flakes easily with a fork, 20 to 25 minutes.

6 Serve immediately, garnished with the parsley.

Crispy Buttermilk
Fried Chicken (page 137)

Chapter Seven

Poultry Mains

Lebanese Baked Lemon Chicken and Rice

SERVES 4 TO 6 · PREP: 15 MINUTES, PLUS 10 MINUTES TO REST CHICKEN · COOK: 1 HOUR & 15 MINUTES

ONE POT

3 lemons, divided

4 tablespoons olive oil, divided

½ teaspoon ground turmeric

1¾ teaspoons kosher salt, divided

Freshly ground black pepper

6 bone-in, skin-on chicken thighs

2 shallots, thinly sliced

½ cup water

1 cup long-grain rice

2¼ cups chicken broth

1 tablespoon dried oregano

2 sprigs fresh rosemary

2 sprigs fresh thyme

¼ cup chopped flat-leaf parsley, for garnish

I'm honestly not sure if this dish is actually Lebanese, but many years before we met, my husband had something similar at the home of some Lebanese friends and craved it forever after. My husband described this dish to me repeatedly over many years until one day I finally did some research on Lebanese cuisine and attempted to re-create it. It's been a favorite in our home ever since.

1 Preheat the oven to 350°F.

2 Zest and juice one of the lemons. Put the zest in a small dish, cover, and set aside for serving.

3 In a large bowl, stir together the juice of the zested lemon, 2 tablespoons of olive oil, the turmeric, 1½ teaspoons of salt, and season with pepper. Add the chicken and turn to coat. Set aside to marinate for about 10 minutes.

4 In the Dutch oven, heat 1 tablespoon of oil over medium-high heat. When the oil is hot, remove the chicken from the marinade and cook in batches, starting with the skin-side down, until browned on both sides, 3 to 4 minutes per side. Transfer the browned chicken to a bowl.

5 Drain the fat from the pot and scrape out any blackened bits. Add the remaining 1 tablespoon of oil to the pot and heat over medium-high heat.

6 Slice the ends off of the two remaining lemons and then slice them into ¼-inch-thick rounds. Remove the seeds. Add the lemon slices to the pot in a single layer and cook, without disturbing them, until browned on the bottom, about 4 minutes. Flip the slices over and continue to cook until browned on the second side, about 3 minutes more. Transfer the lemon slices to a bowl.

7 Add the shallots to the pot and cook, stirring frequently, until softened, about 5 minutes.

8 Add the water to the pot and cook, stirring and scraping up any browned bits from the bottom of the pot. Add the rice, broth, oregano, and the remaining ¼ teaspoon of salt and stir to mix. Bring the liquid to a simmer and then arrange the chicken thighs on top of the rice and layer the lemon slices on top of the chicken. Top with the rosemary and thyme sprigs. Cover and bake for 35 minutes. Uncover and continue to bake for another 10 minutes.

9 Remove the pot from the oven and let rest for 10 minutes before serving. Remove and discard the rosemary and thyme sprigs.

10 Serve hot, garnished with the parsley and the reserved lemon zest.

Chicken Braised with Caramelized Onions and Fennel

SERVES 4 TO 6 • PREP: 10 MINUTES • COOK: 40 MINUTES

2 large fennel bulbs, fronds trimmed and reserved, bulbs halved and very thinly sliced

1 garlic clove, chopped

½ teaspoon grated lemon zest

1 teaspoon kosher salt, divided

⅓ cup olive oil, plus 2 tablespoons

6 (about 1¼ pounds) boneless chicken thighs

½ teaspoon freshly ground black pepper

½ teaspoon fennel seeds

1 onion, thinly sliced

1 tablespoon dry white wine

1 tablespoon freshly squeezed lemon juice

This simple braise capitalizes on the intriguing flavor of fennel by using the bulb, the wispy fronds, and the seeds. The bulb is caramelized along with sliced onion for a deep, vegetal sweetness, while the seeds add a hint of intense licorice flavor, and the puréed fronds add a fresh, herby element. If you want even more of that flavor, substitute Pernod for the wine.

1 In a blender or food processor, combine ½ cup of fennel fronds, the garlic, the lemon zest, and ¼ teaspoon of salt until minced. Add ⅓ cup of oil and process to a smooth purée. Set aside.

2 Season the chicken thighs with ½ teaspoon of salt and ¼ teaspoon of pepper.

3 In the Dutch oven, heat the remaining 2 tablespoons of oil over high heat and cook the chicken, starting with the skin-side down, until nicely browned, about 4 minutes per side. Remove the chicken from the pot and set aside.

4 Add the fennel seeds to the fat in the pot and cook, stirring, for about 30 seconds. Stir in the sliced fennel bulb and onion and season with the remaining ¼ teaspoon of salt and remaining ¼ teaspoon of pepper. Reduce the heat to medium and cook, stirring now and then, until the fennel and onion is well caramelized, about 20 minutes.

5 Deglaze the pan with the wine and cook for 1 to 2 minutes, stirring and scraping up any browned bits from the bottom of the pot, until most of the liquid has evaporated.

6 Arrange the chicken on top of the vegetables in the pot. Add about ¼ cup of water, cover, and reduce the heat to medium-low. Cook for about 10 minutes, until the chicken is cooked through. Remove the lid and cook until all the liquid has cooked off.

7 Add the lemon juice and serve immediately, garnished with the puréed fennel frond mixture.

Creamy Chicken Marsala with Pancetta and Grapes

SERVES 8 • PREP: 10 MINUTES • COOK: 2 HOURS & 45 MINUTES

ONE POT

2 tablespoons
   unsalted butter

2 tablespoons olive oil,
   divided

4 ounces pancetta, diced

8 medium bone-in, skinless
   chicken thighs

Kosher salt

Freshly ground
   black pepper

½ cup all-purpose flour

6 small shallots, halved

2 garlic cloves, thinly sliced

6 sprigs fresh oregano

2 bay leaves

2¼ cups Marsala wine,
   divided

½ cup mascarpone cheese

2 teaspoons cornstarch

8 ounces seedless
   grapes, halved

¼ cup chopped flat-leaf
   parsley, for garnish

Chicken Marsala, that old standby of Italian family restaurants, gets a new twist. Instead of being prepared in a skillet on the stove top using boneless fillets, this version includes meaty thighs slow cooked in the oven. Sweet grapes replace the more standard mushrooms for an updated flavor.

1 Preheat the oven to 275°F.

2 In the Dutch oven, heat the butter and 1 tablespoon of oil over medium heat. Add the pancetta and cook, stirring, until it just begins to brown, about 2 minutes. Using a slotted spoon, transfer the pancetta to a paper towel–lined plate.

3 Add the remaining 1 tablespoon of oil to the pot. Season the chicken with salt and pepper and dredge it in the flour, then sear it in the pot until golden brown on both sides, about 4 minutes per side (you'll probably need to brown the chicken in two batches to avoid crowding the pot). Remove the chicken from the pot and set aside.

4 Add the shallots, garlic, oregano, bay leaves, and 2 cups of Marsala wine to the pot. Bring to a boil over medium-high heat. Reduce the heat to medium and simmer until the liquid is reduced and thickened, about 8 minutes.

5 Return the chicken to the pot, cover, and transfer to the oven. Cook for 2 hours.

6 In a small bowl, stir together the mascarpone cheese, cornstarch, and the remaining ¼ cup of Marsala wine. Add the grapes and the mascarpone cheese mixture to the pot, cover again, and continue to cook in the oven for another 25 to 30 minutes, until the chicken is cooked through.

7 Serve hot, garnished with parsley.

Roasted Whole Chicken with Lemon, Garlic, and Herbs

SERVES 4–6 • PREP: 10 MINUTES, PLUS 10 MINUTES TO REST CHICKEN • COOK: 1 HOUR & 5 MINUTES

ONE POT

4 tablespoons
    unsalted butter

2 lemons, both zested,
    juiced, and remaining
    rinds reserved

5 garlic cloves, 3 minced,
    2 halved

4 sprigs fresh rosemary,
    3 finely chopped,
    1 full

Kosher salt

Freshly ground
    black pepper

2 large onions, sliced
    into thick rings

1 whole chicken (3 to
    4 pounds), rinsed
    and patted dry

A simple roast chicken is a beautiful thing. It makes a wonderful Sunday family dinner, plus there are always leftovers to be transformed into new dishes. A Dutch oven is perfect for roasting a whole chicken. For one thing, an average-size chicken fits nicely into a 5½-quart Dutch oven, and because the sides of the pot radiate heat just as the bottom does, the chicken gets evenly roasted, plus the skin gets nice and crisp.

1 Preheat the oven to 475°F.

2 In a small bowl, melt the butter in the microwave. Stir in the lemon zest, minced garlic, chopped rosemary, and pinches of salt and pepper.

3 Spread the onion rings on the bottom of the Dutch oven.

4 Season the chicken liberally with salt and pepper, both inside and outside.

5 Use your hands to coat the chicken generously with the butter mixture, including underneath the skin of the breast (being careful not to tear the skin). Put the lemon rinds inside the cavity of the chicken along with the remaining rosemary sprig. Place the chicken in the Dutch oven on top of the onions and drizzle the lemon juice over the top.

6 Roast the chicken uncovered for 15 minutes, and then reduce the heat to 350°F and cook for another 40 to 50 minutes, basting the chicken with its juices halfway through.

7 Remove the chicken from the oven and transfer it from the pot to a cutting board. Tent it loosely with foil and let it rest for 10 minutes before carving. Serve immediately or refrigerate for up to 3 days.

Essential Technique: It's best to leave the lid off of the pot while roasting the chicken. This allows moisture to escape and the skin to become crisp. However, if your chicken seems to be browning too quickly on top, set the lid on top, slightly ajar. This will slow down the browning while still letting moisture escape.

Chicken Tagine with Dried Apricots

SERVES 6 • PREP: 10 MINUTES • COOK: 1 HOUR

1 teaspoon cinnamon

1 teaspoon ground ginger

½ teaspoon turmeric

½ teaspoon freshly ground black pepper

1¼ teaspoons kosher salt, divided

3 tablespoons olive oil

1 whole chicken (about 3 pounds), cut into 6 pieces, wings and backbone discarded

1 tablespoon unsalted butter

1 onion, halved and sliced ¼ inch thick

4 garlic cloves, minced

4 sprigs cilantro

4 sprigs flat-leaf parsley

1½ cups water

2 tablespoons honey

1 cinnamon stick

½ cup halved dried apricots

¼ cup chopped cilantro, for garnish

A true tagine is a spiced North African stew cooked in an eponymous earthenware pot—a shallow pot with a flat, wide base and a tall, conical lid that provides a uniquely hot and moist cooking environment. A Dutch oven works on much the same principle and produces delicious spiced stews in the style of North African tagines. This chicken version is studded with plump, sweet apricots and spiced with cinnamon, ginger, and turmeric. Serve it over couscous.

1 In a large bowl, whisk together the cinnamon, ginger, turmeric, pepper, 1 teaspoon of salt, and 2 tablespoons of oil. Add the chicken pieces to the bowl and turn so that each piece is well coated with the spice mixture.

2 In the Dutch oven, heat the butter and the remaining 1 tablespoon of oil over medium heat. Add the chicken pieces (brown in two batches to avoid crowding the pot) and cook, beginning with the skin-side down, until browned on both sides, about 4 minutes per side. As the chicken pieces are browned, transfer them to a plate.

3 Add the onion and the remaining ¼ teaspoon of salt to the pot and cook, stirring often, for about 5 minutes, until the onion is softened.

4 Stir in the garlic and cook, stirring, for 2 minutes more. Return the browned chicken to the pot, along with any juices that have accumulated on the plate, and add the sprigs of cilantro and parsley, and ½ cup of water. Cover the pot, reduce the heat to medium-low, and simmer for 20 minutes.

5 Meanwhile, in a medium saucepan, combine the remaining 1 cup of water with the honey, cinnamon stick, and apricots and bring to a boil. Reduce the heat and simmer, uncovered, until the apricots have softened and the liquid has thickened to a syrupy consistency, about 20 minutes.

6 Stir in the apricot mixture to the chicken and cook, covered, for 10 minutes more. Remove and discard the herb sprigs and cinnamon stick.

7 Serve hot, garnished with cilantro.

Chicken, Leek, and Mushroom Pot Pie

SERVES 8 · PREP: 25 MINUTES · COOK: 1 HOUR & 10 MINUTES

FOR THE CRUST

1½ cups all-purpose flour

¼ teaspoon fine sea salt

¼ teaspoon baking powder

½ cup (1 stick) unsalted butter, chilled and cut into small pieces

1 teaspoon white or cider vinegar

4 to 5 tablespoons ice water

Chicken pot pie is the very definition of comfort food. Using the Dutch oven, you can cook the filling and the assembled pie all in one pot, making cleanup a breeze. This version is filled with plump cooked chicken, succulent mushrooms, and flavorful leeks in a rich gravy. The buttery, flaky crust is easy to make, but if you're short on time, feel free to use a store-bought crust.

TO MAKE THE CRUST

1 In a large bowl or food processor, combine the flour, salt, and baking powder. Using a pastry cutter, two knives, or the S blade of your food processor, cut the butter into the dry ingredients until the mixture forms coarse crumbs with some pea-size lumps.

2 In a small bowl, stir together the vinegar and 4 tablespoons of water. Sprinkle the vinegar mixture over the flour and butter mixture and stir, process, or mix with your hands just until the mixture comes together. If necessary to bring the dough together, add up to 1 additional tablespoon of water.

3 Shape the dough into a round disk, wrap it tightly in plastic wrap, and chill it in the refrigerator while you make the filling.

FOR THE FILLING

1 tablespoon olive oil

7 tablespoons unsalted
butter, divided

2 carrots, diced

2 celery stalks, diced

1 large leek, trimmed, halved
lengthwise, and sliced

Kosher salt

1 pound button or cremini
mushrooms, sliced

Freshly ground
black pepper

½ cup dry white wine

6 tablespoons all-purpose
flour, plus more for
dusting the work surface

1½ cups chicken broth

1 cup whole milk

6 cups (about 2 pounds)
diced cooked chicken

1 teaspoon minced
fresh thyme

FOR ASSEMBLING
THE POT PIE

1 large egg, beaten with
1 teaspoon warm water

TO MAKE THE FILLING

1 Preheat the oven to 400°F.

2 In the Dutch oven, heat the oil and 1 tablespoon of butter over medium heat. Add the carrots, celery, and leek, season with a pinch of salt, and cook, stirring occasionally, until the vegetables soften, about 15 minutes. Using a slotted spoon, transfer the carrot and leek mixture to a bowl.

3 Add 1 tablespoon of butter and the mushrooms to the pot and season with a pinch of salt and pepper. Cook, stirring frequently, until the mushrooms are softened and beginning to brown, about 8 minutes.

4 Add the wine and bring to a boil. Cook, stirring and scraping up any browned bits from the bottom of the pot, until the liquid has evaporated, about 2 minutes. Transfer the mushrooms to the bowl with the carrots and leeks.

5 Add the remaining 5 tablespoons of butter to the pot and melt over medium heat. Sprinkle the flour over the melted butter and whisk to combine. Cook, whisking constantly, until the mixture is smooth and turns a pale golden brown, about 5 minutes. >>

6 Whisk in the chicken broth and milk until well combined.

7 Return the vegetable mixture to the pot, add the chicken and thyme, and stir to mix. Taste and adjust the seasoning if needed.

TO ASSEMBLE THE POT PIE

Roll out the pie dough to an even thickness and slightly larger in diameter than the Dutch oven. Lay the pie dough over the top of the filling, tucking the excess underneath so that it fits snugly just inside the rim of the pot. Slash several vents into the crust with a sharp knife to allow steam to escape. Brush the top with the egg and water wash. Bake for about 40 minutes, until the pastry puffs up and turns golden brown.

Essential Technique: This recipe calls for cooked chicken. You can use leftover roasted or rotisserie chicken or quickly poach some chicken just for this dish. Bring a saucepan filled about 3 inches deep with water to a simmer. Add about 2 pounds of boneless, skinless chicken (thighs or breasts) and simmer gently until the chicken is opaque and just cooked through, 10 to 15 minutes.

Crispy Buttermilk Fried Chicken

SERVES 6 • PREP: 5 MINUTES, PLUS 30 MINUTES TO MARINATE • COOK: 40 MINUTES

ONE POT

2 cups buttermilk

2 teaspoons kosher salt, divided

1 teaspoon cayenne pepper, divided

1 teaspoon garlic powder, divided

1 teaspoon paprika, divided

1 (3- to 4-pound) whole chicken, cut into 8 pieces

4 cups vegetable oil, for frying

1½ cups all-purpose flour

Essential Technique: Very hot oil is essential for crispy, nongreasy fried chicken. A deep-fry thermometer can help ensure that your oil gets to, and stays at, the right temperature. If you don't have one, test your oil by sprinkling in a bit of flour. If the oil is hot enough, the flour will sizzle immediately and dissipate quickly.

Marinating chicken pieces in spiced buttermilk not only infuses them with flavor but also ensures that the meat will be super tender. A quick flour-and-spice coating adds additional flavor and makes a crisp, crunchy crust once it's fried. Using the Dutch oven as a deep-fryer helps to contain splatters so you don't make a complete mess of your stove top.

1 In a large bowl, combine the buttermilk, 1 teaspoon of salt, ¼ teaspoon of cayenne, ¼ teaspoon of garlic powder, and ¼ teaspoon of paprika. Add the chicken and toss to coat. Cover and chill in the refrigerator for at least 30 minutes (or as long as overnight).

2 Fill the Dutch oven about half full with vegetable oil and heat it over medium-high heat until the oil registers 360°F on a deep-fry thermometer.

3 While the oil is heating, combine the flour, the remaining 1 teaspoon of salt, the remaining ¾ teaspoon of cayenne, the remaining ¾ teaspoon of garlic powder, and the remaining ¾ teaspoon of paprika in a shallow, wide bowl.

4 To cook the chicken, remove it from the marinade, letting the excess run off, and dredge it in the flour mixture. Lower the chicken into the hot oil and cook, turning occasionally, until the chicken is golden brown on the outside and cooked through, about 15 minutes. Cook the chicken a few pieces at a time, being careful not to crowd the pot or cause the oil's temperature to drop. As the chicken pieces are finished cooking, transfer them to a wire rack or paper towel–lined platter.

5 Serve hot or at room temperature.

Chicken and Vegetables Braised in Vinegar

SERVES 4 TO 6 • PREP: 10 MINUTES • COOK: 1 HOUR

ONE POT

2 tablespoons olive oil,
    divided

6 ounces pancetta, diced

4 small shallots, halved or
    quartered

6 ounces small button or
    cremini mushrooms

4 garlic cloves

4 pounds skin-on bone-in
    chicken pieces (breasts,
    thighs, and/or legs)

Kosher salt

Freshly ground
    black pepper

⅔ cup balsamic vinegar

⅔ cup red wine vinegar

1½ cups low-sodium
    chicken broth

6 small carrots, peeled
    and cut into sticks

2 small parsnips, peeled
    and cut into sticks

2 bay leaves

Braising chicken in a mixture of balsamic and wine vinegars pierces it with sweet-tart flavor that is perfectly addictive. Salty pancetta and aromatic shallots and garlic add nuanced levels of flavor, too. Serve this dish with a crisp salad and roasted potatoes for a special family meal.

1 In the Dutch oven, heat 1 tablespoon of oil over medium heat. Add the pancetta and cook, stirring frequently, about 5 minutes, until browned. Using a slotted spoon, transfer the pancetta to a large bowl.

2 Add the shallots and the mushrooms to the Dutch oven and cook, stirring frequently, until they begin to brown, about 5 minutes.

3 Stir in the garlic and cook, stirring, for about 1 more minute. Using a slotted spoon, transfer the shallots, mushrooms, and garlic to the bowl of pancetta. **>>**

4 Season the chicken generously with salt and pepper. Add the remaining 1 tablespoon of oil to the pot and cook the chicken, beginning with the skin-side down, until it is browned on both sides, about 4 minutes per side (brown in two batches to avoid crowding the pot). As the chicken pieces are browned, transfer them to the bowl with the pancetta and shallots.

5 Drain the fat from the pot. Combine the balsamic and wine vinegars in the pot and bring to a boil over medium-high heat, deglazing the pot and scraping up any browned bits from bottom of the pot. Stir in the broth, carrots, parsnips, and bay leaves, and return the chicken, pancetta, and vegetables to the pot. When the mixture comes to a boil, reduce the heat to medium. Set the lid ajar and simmer for about 40 minutes, until the chicken is very tender. Remove and discard the bay leaves and adjust the seasoning if needed.

6 Serve the chicken hot with the sauce spooned over it.

Spicy Indian Butter Chicken

SERVES 4 • PREP: 10 MINUTES, PLUS 30 MINUTES TO MARINATE • COOK: 30 MINUTES

ONE POT

FOR THE MARINADE

½ cup plain yogurt

1 tablespoon lemon juice

2 teaspoons garam masala

1 teaspoon ground cumin

1 teaspoon turmeric

½ teaspoon cayenne pepper

2 garlic cloves, crushed

1 tablespoon grated
fresh ginger

1½ pounds boneless,
skinless chicken
thighs, cubed

FOR THE CURRY

1 tablespoon vegetable oil

1 tablespoon
unsalted butter

1 tablespoon grated
fresh ginger

1 garlic clove, minced

1 (14.5-ounce) can
crushed tomatoes

1 tablespoon sugar

1¼ teaspoons kosher salt

1 teaspoon garam masala

½ cup heavy cream

¼ cup chopped cilantro,
for garnish

Butter chicken is an Indian restaurant take-out favorite, but this version is so easy you'll want to make it at home all the time. Marinating the chicken in a spiced yogurt mixture makes it super tender and infuses it with intense flavor. You can find garam masala in the spice aisle of most supermarkets or online. Serve this saucy chicken dish over rice or with naan or another flatbread for dunking.

TO MAKE THE MARINADE

In a large bowl, stir together the yogurt, lemon juice, garam masala, cumin, turmeric, cayenne, garlic, and ginger. Add the chicken and toss to coat. Cover and refrigerate for at least 30 minutes (or as long as overnight).

TO MAKE THE CURRY

1 In the Dutch oven, heat the vegetable oil and butter over high heat. Add the ginger and garlic and cook, stirring, until softened, about 1 minute.

2 Add the marinated chicken and cook until the chicken turns opaque, about 5 minutes.

3 Stir in the tomatoes, sugar, salt, and garam masala. Reduce the heat to low and simmer until the chicken is cooked through, about 20 minutes.

4 Stir in the cream and serve hot, garnished with the cilantro.

Chicken Paprikash

SERVES 8 • PREP: 10 MINUTES • COOK: 1 HOUR

ONE POT

3 to 4 pounds chicken
thighs or drumsticks
(or a mix of the two)

Kosher salt

Freshly ground
black pepper

1 tablespoon vegetable oil

1 tablespoons
unsalted butter

1 onion, diced

3 garlic cloves, minced

3 tablespoons sweet or hot
Hungarian paprika (or a
combination of the two)

3 tablespoons
all-purpose flour

1 cup canned crushed
tomatoes

1 cup chicken broth

¾ cup sour cream

Egg noodles, cooked
according to package
directions

¼ cup chopped fresh
flat-leafed parsley,
for garnish

Chicken paprikash is one of the world's best-known and best-loved peasant dishes. Chicken pieces are browned in butter and cooked with onions and lots of Hungarian paprika (you can use sweet or hot paprika, or a mixture if you like). In some versions (like this one), sour cream is stirred into the sauce at the end. To be truly authentic, serve it over dumplings or buttered egg noodles.

1 Preheat the oven to 400°F.

2 Generously season the chicken with salt and pepper.

3 In the Dutch oven, heat the oil and 1 tablespoon of butter over high heat. When the butter begins to foam, add the chicken (brown in two batches to avoid crowding the pan), beginning with the skin-side down, until browned on both sides, about 4 minutes per side. As the chicken pieces are browned, transfer them to a plate.

4 Drain all but 2 tablespoons of fat from the Dutch oven and set it over medium heat. Add the onion and cook, stirring frequently, until softened, about 5 minutes.

5 Stir in the garlic and cook, stirring, for 1 minute more. Sprinkle the paprika and flour over the onion and cook, stirring, for about 5 minutes, until the flour releases a nutty aroma.

6 Stir in the tomatoes and broth and cook, whisking constantly, until the sauce is well combined.

7 Return the chicken to the pot with the skin side up. Transfer to the oven and bake for about 30 minutes, until the chicken is cooked through and the sauce thickens.

8 Remove the chicken from the pot and stir in the sour cream until it is well combined.

9 Serve the chicken over cooked egg noodles, with the sauce spooned over the top and garnished with parsley.

Did You Know? Paprika is associated most closely with Hungary, but the peppers it is made from originated, like all peppers, in the New World. The peppers have been grown in southern Hungary for at least 500 years and have become an integral ingredient in the region's cuisine. Once dried and ground, the peppers lose their flavor in short order, so do yourself a favor and make lots of paprikash so you can use up that tin of paprika before it's too late.

Turkey Shepherd's Pie with Sweet Potato Topping

SERVES 6 TO 8 • PREP: 10 MINUTES • COOK: 1 HOUR & 15 MINUTES

2 ½ pounds sweet potatoes,
    peeled and cut
    into cubes

Kosher salt

4 tablespoons butter,
    divided

3 carrots, peeled and diced

2 celery stalks, diced

1 onion, diced

2 tablespoons chopped
    fresh thyme

2 pounds turkey, cooked
    and chopped

¼ cup tomato paste

2 tablespoons
    all-purpose flour

2 tablespoons
    Worcestershire sauce

2 cups chicken broth

½ cup heavy cream

Freshly ground
    black pepper

This simple savory casserole is a great way to use up leftover Thanksgiving turkey, but you could also substitute cooked chicken. Serve it with Bourbon-Spiked Cranberry Sauce (page 62) and green beans in melted butter, and it'll be like Thanksgiving no matter what day it is.

1 Preheat the oven to 375°F.

2 In a large saucepan, place the sweet potatoes and cover with water. Add a generous pinch of salt. Set the saucepan over medium-high heat and bring to a simmer. Reduce the heat to medium and simmer for about 20 minutes, until the potatoes are tender.

3 Meanwhile, in the Dutch oven, melt 2 tablespoons of butter over medium-high heat. Add the carrots, celery, and onion and cook, stirring frequently, until the vegetables are softened, about 12 minutes.

4 Stir in the thyme, turkey, tomato paste, flour, and Worcestershire sauce. Add the broth, bring to a simmer, and cook over medium heat until the sauce has thickened, about 5 minutes.

5 When the potatoes are done, drain them and transfer them to a large bowl. Add the remaining 2 tablespoons of butter, the cream, and season with salt and pepper. Mash the potatoes with a potato masher until well combined.

6 In the Dutch oven, spread the turkey mixture into an even layer and top with the mashed sweet potato mixture. Transfer to the oven and bake for about 35 minutes, until the top is lightly browned. Serve hot.

Duck and Sausage Cassoulet

SERVES 4 • PREP: 20 MINUTES, PLUS 8 HOURS TO SOAK THE BEANS • COOK: 2 HOURS & 10 MINUTES

ONE POT

FOR THE STEW

½ pound bacon, diced

4 duck legs

Kosher salt

Freshly ground
    black pepper

4 uncooked sausages
    (preferably a variety with
    lots of garlic and spices)

1 large onion, diced

6 garlic cloves, minced

1 celery stalk, chopped

1 tablespoon tomato paste

1 (14.5-oz) can stewed
    tomatoes, puréed or
    finely chopped

1 pound dried white beans
    (such as great northern
    or cannellini), soaked
    for at least 8 hours
    and then drained

3 fresh thyme sprigs

3 flat-leaf parsley sprigs

1 bay leaf

3 whole cloves

¼ teaspoon whole black
    peppercorns

There are many traditional versions of cassoulet, the classic slow-cooked French white bean stew topped with rich meats and a crunchy baked-on crust, with the versions varying depending on which town in France they originated in. All of them include white beans stewed with rich meats like duck, bacon or salt pork, and sausages. This version is simplified but no less delicious than the classic ones.

TO MAKE THE STEW

1 Preheat the oven to 400°F.

2 In the Dutch oven, cook the bacon, stirring frequently, over medium-high heat until browned, about 4 minutes. Using a slotted spoon, transfer the bacon to a paper towel–lined plate.

3 Season the duck legs generously with salt and pepper. Add the duck legs to the Dutch oven and cook, turning once, until well browned on both sides, about 5 minutes per side (you may have to cook the duck legs in two batches to avoid crowding the pan). Transfer the duck legs to the plate with the bacon. Drain and reserve most of the fat from the pot.

4 Add the sausages to the Dutch oven and cook, turning occasionally, until browned on all sides, about 6 minutes. Transfer the sausages to the plate with the duck and bacon. Again, drain most of the fat from the pot, leaving just about 2 tablespoons for sautéing the vegetables.

FOR THE BREAD CRUMB TOPPING

2 cups coarse fresh bread crumbs

2 garlic cloves, minced

½ cup minced flat-leaf parsley

1½ teaspoons kosher salt

½ teaspoon freshly ground black pepper

6 tablespoons unsalted butter, melted

Essential Technique: If you've forgotten to soak your beans overnight, you can still pull off this recipe today. Rinse the beans and put them in your Dutch oven and cover with about 2 inches of water. Bring to a boil over high heat. Remove the pot from the heat, cover, and let the beans soak for 1 hour. Drain the beans and proceed with the recipe.

5 Add the onion, garlic, and celery to the pot and cook, stirring frequently, until softened and beginning to brown, about 10 minutes.

6 Stir in the tomato paste and cook for about 2 minutes more. Add the tomatoes and beans and enough water to cover the beans completely. Bring to a boil. Add the browned bacon and stir to mix well. Place the duck legs and sausages in the pot atop the beans.

7 Wrap the thyme and parsley sprigs, the bay leaf, cloves, and peppercorns in a piece of cheesecloth and tie with a piece of kitchen twine, making a bouquet garni. Tuck this bundle into the Dutch oven. Cover the pot and bake for about 1½ hours, until the beans are tender and the duck legs are cooked through.

TO MAKE THE BREAD CRUMB TOPPING

1 In a medium bowl, stir together the bread crumbs, garlic, parsley, salt, pepper, and melted butter.

2 Remove the Dutch oven from the oven and reduce the heat to 350°F. Fish the bouquet garni out of the stew and discard it. Spread the bread crumb mixture evenly over the top of the stew and return the pot to the oven. Cook, uncovered, for about 10 minutes more, until the topping is crisp and nicely browned. Serve hot.

Short Ribs Braised in
Red Wine (page 166)

Chapter Eight

Pork, Beef & Lamb Mains

Roasted Chipotle-Orange Pork Tenderloin

SERVES 4 TO 6 • PREP: 20 MINUTES, PLUS 1 HOUR TO MARINATE • COOK: 30 MINUTES

2 canned chipotle chiles in adobo plus 1 tablespoon of adobo sauce

2 garlic cloves, minced

1 shallot

1 cup orange juice

6 tablespoons lime juice

2 tablespoons red wine vinegar

2 teaspoons dried oregano

1 teaspoon ground cumin

½ teaspoon kosher salt, plus additional for seasoning

½ teaspoon freshly ground black pepper, plus additional for seasoning

2 pork tenderloins (about 1 pound each), halved crosswise

2 tablespoons olive oil

¾ cup chicken broth

Pork tenderloin is quick to cook. This spicy and citrusy marinade gives it great flavor. It's delicious on its own with roasted potatoes or rice, but it also makes a great filling for tacos. Pork tenderloin is leaner than other pork cuts, so it makes for the kind of lighter meal you crave in the summertime.

1 In a blender or food processor, combine the chipotles and sauce, garlic, shallot, orange juice, lime juice, vinegar, oregano, cumin, ½ teaspoon of salt, and ½ teaspoon of pepper and process until smooth. Place the pork in a large bowl or a large resealable plastic bag and pour the marinade over it, tossing to coat well. Cover or seal and marinate in the refrigerator for 1 hour (or as long as overnight).

2 Preheat the oven to 400°F.

3 In the Dutch oven, heat the oil. Remove the meat from the marinade, reserving the marinade, and pat dry with paper towels. Season the pork with additional salt and pepper. Add the pork to the Dutch oven and sear on all sides, about 5 minutes total.

4 Transfer the Dutch oven to the oven and roast, uncovered, for about 12 minutes, until the pork is cooked through (it should register 145°F on an instant-read thermometer.) Remove the tenderloins from the Dutch oven, transfer to a cutting board, and cover with foil. Let rest for at least 10 minutes.

5 Meanwhile, add the reserved marinade to the Dutch oven, stir in the broth, and set over high heat. Bring to a boil and cook, stirring occasionally, until the sauce has thickened, about 10 minutes.

6 Slice the pork into ¼-inch-thick slices and serve, drizzled with the sauce.

Did You Know? Chipotle chiles in adobo sauce are dried and smoked jalapeño chiles that come in a can packed in adobo sauce—a tangy-sweet tomato sauce. You can usually find them in the international foods aisle of the supermarket or at Mexican grocers. If you can't find them, substitute ½ teaspoon of ground chipotle or regular chili powder.

Carnitas Tacos

SERVES 8 • PREP: 15 MINUTES • COOK: 1 HOUR & 50 MINUTES

FOR THE CARNITAS

4 pounds bone-in
  pork butt, cut into
  2-inch-thick slabs

1 teaspoon kosher salt

⅓ cup water

FOR THE PICKLED ONIONS

1 large red onion, halved
  and thinly sliced

1½ teaspoons kosher salt

½ cup lime juice (from
  about 6 limes)

FOR THE TACOS

16 corn tortillas, warmed

1 cup salsa

½ head green cabbage,
  shredded

Carnitas is essentially a Mexican version of pork confit—meaty pork slow-cooked until it is fall-apart tender. This quicker version combines braising and slow roasting, producing succulent chunks of pork with delectably crunchy edges, ideal for filling tacos.

TO MAKE THE CARNITAS

1 Preheat the oven to 375°F.

2 Season the pork slabs on all sides with the salt. Pour ⅓ cup of water in the bottom of the Dutch oven, arrange the meat in the pot in a single layer, if possible. Cover and bake for 1 hour.

3 Remove the lid from the pot and increase the oven temperature to 450°F. Roast uncovered until the water is completely evaporated and the fat has rendered from the meat, about 30 minutes.

4 Continue to roast, turning the meat a few times over the next 20 to 25 minutes, until the meat falls apart. Remove the meat from the oven and shred it with two forks, removing and discarding the bones.

TO MAKE THE PICKLED ONIONS

In a large heatproof bowl, add the sliced onions and pour boiling water over them. Let sit for about 20 seconds and then drain in a colander. Transfer the onions to a bowl, stir in the salt and lime juice, and let sit for at least 30 minutes.

TO ASSEMBLE THE TACOS

Place some of the meat down the center of each of the tortillas. Top with a bunch of pickled onions, a spoonful of salsa, and a handful of cabbage. Serve immediately.

Smoked Pork and Sausage Jambalaya

SERVES 6 • PREP: 15 MINUTES • COOK: 40 MINUTES

ONE POT

2 tablespoons
  unsalted butter

2 pounds smoked pork loin,
  cut into cubes

12 ounces Andouille
  sausage, sliced

2 medium onions, diced

2 green bell peppers, diced

4 celery stalks, diced

½ teaspoon salt

½ teaspoon pepper

6 garlic cloves, minced

2 bay leaves

¼ to ½ teaspoon cayenne
  pepper

1 (28-ounce) can diced
  tomatoes

1 cup long-grain white rice

2 cups water

1 pound peeled and
  deveined shrimp

4 scallions, thinly sliced,
  for garnish

This flavorful stew has all the marks of Cajun cooking: smoky meat, spicy sausage, and, of course, the holy trinity (onion, bell peppers, and celery). If you don't have smoked pork loin, you can substitute slow-cooked pork butt or shoulder, or even another meat like chicken.

1 Preheat the oven to 350°F.

2 In the Dutch oven, melt the butter over medium-high heat. Add the smoked pork and the sausage to the pot and cook, stirring frequently, until browned, about 5 minutes. Transfer the meat to a bowl.

3 Add the onions, bell peppers, celery, salt, and pepper to the pot and cook, stirring occasionally, until the vegetables soften, about 8 minutes.

4 Add the garlic, bay leaves, and cayenne and cook, stirring, for about 6 minutes more, until the vegetables are golden brown.

5 Stir in the tomatoes, rice, water, and reserved pork and sausage and bring to a boil. Reduce the heat to medium and simmer, uncovered, until the rice is tender, about 20 minutes.

6 Stir in the shrimp and cook until the shrimp are cooked through, 3 to 4 minutes more.

7 Taste and season the jambalaya if needed. Serve hot, garnished with the scallions.

White Bean Stew with Spanish Chorizo

SERVES 4 • PREP: 10 MINUTES • COOK: 45 MINUTES

ONE POT

3 tablespoons olive oil, divided, plus more for drizzling

3 links (about 12 ounces) Spanish chorizo, sliced

1 onion, diced

4 garlic cloves, minced

2 sprigs fresh thyme

1 tablespoon paprika

1 bay leaf

½ teaspoon cayenne pepper

½ teaspoon kosher salt

¼ teaspoon freshly ground black pepper

2 (15-ounce) cans cannellini beans, drained and rinsed

2 cups chicken broth

1 tablespoon sherry vinegar

2 cups panko bread crumbs

½ cup grated Parmesan cheese

¼ cup chopped flat-leaf parsley, for garnish

I could easily eat this hearty stew once a week. It's got everything I love in a one-pot meal—healthy beans, a bit of flavorful meat, and crunchy bread crumbs, plus a broth that is delicious sopped up with crusty bread. When I'm in the mood for soup, I just add a few additional cups of broth.

1 Preheat the oven to 400°F.

2 In the Dutch oven, heat 1 tablespoon of oil over medium heat. Add the chorizo and cook, stirring occasionally, until browned, about 10 minutes. Using a slotted spoon, transfer the sausage to a plate.

3 Add 1 tablespoon of oil to the Dutch oven and heat over medium heat. Add the onion, garlic, and thyme, and cook, stirring frequently, until the onion softens, about 5 minutes. Stir in the chorizo, paprika, bay leaf, cayenne, salt, pepper, beans, broth, and vinegar.

4 In a small bowl, stir together the bread crumbs, Parmesan cheese, and the remaining 1 tablespoon of olive oil. Sprinkle the bread crumb mixture evenly over the beans.

5 Bake, uncovered, in the preheated oven, for about 30 minutes, until the broth is hot and bubbling and the topping is browned and crisp. Remove and discard the bay leaf. Serve hot, garnished with the parsley.

Braised Pork Chops with Vegetables and Thyme

SERVES 4 • PREP: 10 MINUTES • COOK: 30 MINUTES

ONE POT

WEEKNIGHT WIN

4 (1-inch-thick) bone-in pork loin chops

1¾ teaspoons kosher salt, divided

1 teaspoon paprika

2 tablespoons olive oil

1 onion, chopped

2 garlic cloves, thinly sliced

½ teaspoon freshly ground black pepper

2 carrots, peeled and cut into 2-inch sticks

2 celery stalks, cut into 2-inch sticks

1 red bell pepper, seeded and cut into 2-inch slices

½ cup chicken broth

½ cup dry vermouth

3 sprigs fresh thyme

1 teaspoon Dijon mustard

½ teaspoon finely grated lemon zest

1 teaspoon freshly squeezed lemon juice

Pork chops remain juicy and tender when seared in a hot pan and then braised, along with vegetables, in broth and vermouth. This satisfying meal is quick enough to make any night of the week but special enough to serve to guests. If you don't have dry vermouth, substitute a dry white wine.

1 Pat the pork chops dry with paper towels. Season them all over with ¾ teaspoon of salt and the paprika.

2 In the Dutch oven, heat the oil over medium-high heat. Sear the pork chops for about 3 minutes per side, until golden brown (do this in two batches to avoid crowding the pot). As the pork chops are browned, transfer them to a plate.

3 Reduce the heat to medium. Add the onion and garlic, along with the remaining ¾ teaspoon of salt and the pepper. Cook, stirring frequently, until the onion begins to soften, about 3 minutes.

4 Add the carrots, celery, and bell pepper. Stir in the broth and vermouth and cook, stirring and scraping up any browned bits from the bottom of the pot, for about 3 minutes more.

5 Add the browned chops back to the pot, along with any juices that have accumulated and the thyme. Reduce the heat to low, cover, and simmer for about 8 minutes, until the pork chops are cooked through.

6 Transfer the chops to a plate and tent loosely with aluminum foil. Let the meat rest for 10 minutes.

7 While the chops rest, raise the heat under the pot to medium-high and let the sauce simmer, uncovered, for 6 to 8 minutes, until it thickens a bit and the vegetables are tender.

8 Remove the pot from the heat and stir in the mustard and lemon zest and lemon juice. Remove and discard the thyme sprigs.

9 Serve the chops along with the vegetables and sauce.

Roasted Pork Loin with Fennel and Apple Stuffing

SERVES 6 TO 8 • PREP: 20 MINUTES, PLUS 15 MINUTES TO REST PORK • COOK: 1 HOUR & 20 MINUTES

ONE POT

FOR THE STUFFING

1 tablespoon olive oil

1 tablespoon
unsalted butter

2 onions, sliced

1 large bulb fennel, cored
and thinly sliced

2 teaspoons kosher salt

½ teaspoon freshly ground
black pepper

1 large Granny Smith apple,
peeled, cored, and diced

2 garlic cloves, minced

1 tablespoon minced fresh
thyme leaves

1 tablespoon white wine

3 cups fresh bread crumbs

I love this recipe because you can use the same Dutch oven for all three of its parts—to sauté the vegetables and aromatics for the stuffing, to roast the pork, and then to make a pan sauce while the roast is resting. Fennel, apples, and fresh bread crumbs make a delicious filling for juicy pork loin. The apple cider pan sauce is a simple finishing touch that elevates the dish beyond the ordinary.

TO MAKE THE STUFFING

1 Preheat the oven to 425°F.

2 In the Dutch oven, heat the olive oil and butter over medium-high heat. Stir in the onions, fennel, salt, and pepper. Reduce the heat to medium-low and cook, stirring occasionally, until the vegetables have softened and are beginning to brown, about 10 minutes.

3 Stir in the apple and continue to cook, stirring occasionally, for 5 minutes more. Stir in the garlic and thyme and cook, stirring, about 1 minute more. Add the wine to deglaze the pan and cook, stirring, for 1 minute more. Remove from the heat. Stir the bread crumbs into the vegetable mixture.

FOR THE PORK ROAST

1 (3½-pound) pork loin, butterflied

Kosher salt

Freshly ground black pepper

1 tablespoon olive oil

FOR THE PAN SAUCE

4 tablespoons unsalted butter, divided

2 shallots, diced

¾ cup apple cider

½ teaspoon apple cider vinegar

1 tablespoon minced parsley

TO MAKE THE PORK ROAST

1 Lay the pork on a board with the fat-side down. Season with salt and pepper. Spoon the stuffing mixture onto the pork and spread it out into an even layer. Roll the meat up lengthwise and tie it with kitchen twine to hold it together. Drizzle the olive oil over the top and season again with salt and pepper.

2 Wipe out the Dutch oven and place the stuffed roast into it. Roast, uncovered, for 30 minutes and then reduce the heat to 350°F. Continue roasting for 20 to 30 minutes more, until the pork is cooked through (it should register 140°F on an instant-read meat thermometer). Transfer the roast to a cutting board. Cover with aluminum foil and let rest for 15 minutes.

TO MAKE THE PAN SAUCE

1 In the Dutch oven, melt 2 tablespoons of butter over medium-high heat. Add the shallots and cook, stirring, until softened, about 3 minutes.

2 Stir in the apple cider and cook, stirring and scraping up any browned bits from the bottom of the pot, until the liquid is reduced by half.

3 Stir in the cider vinegar and the remaining 2 tablespoons of butter. Swirl until the butter is completely incorporated. Stir in the parsley.

4 To serve, remove the strings and slice the pork into 1½-inch-thick slices. Serve hot, topped with the pan sauce.

Cider-Braised Pork with Apples and Red Cabbage

SERVES 6 • PREP: 10 MINUTES, PLUS 10 MINUTES TO REST PORK • COOK: 55 MINUTES

ONE POT

1 (2½-pound) pork loin

1½ teaspoons salt

½ teaspoon freshly ground black pepper

1 tablespoon unsalted butter

1 tablespoon olive oil

1 onion, diced

3 tart apples, peeled, cored, and cut into wedges

1 head red cabbage, cored and thinly sliced

½ cup apple cider vinegar

1½ cups apple cider

1 cup chicken broth

Perfect Pairing: This meaty meal begs to be paired with a crisp lager-style beer or even a hard cider. If you are more of a wine drinker, a light but rich red, such as pinot noir, would be perfect.

Pork, apples, and cabbage are a perfect match. This simple pork roast is cooked right along with the fruit and vegetables, making the hands-on work minimal. Serve it with roasted or mashed potatoes for a hearty Sunday dinner.

1 Preheat the oven 350°F.

2 Season the pork loin with salt and pepper. In the Dutch oven, heat the butter and oil over medium-high heat. Add the pork and cook, turning occasionally, until it is browned on all sides, about 8 minutes total. Transfer the meat to a bowl.

3 Reduce the heat to medium, add the onion, and cook, stirring occasionally, until softened, about 5 minutes.

4 Add the apples, cabbage, vinegar, cider, and broth and return to a boil over high heat. Reduce the heat to medium, cover, and simmer for 7 minutes.

5 Return the pork to the pot along with any accumulated juices, nestling the roast into the apples and vegetables. Roast, uncovered, for 35 to 40 minutes, until an instant-read thermometer registers 140°F.

6 Transfer the pork to a cutting board, tent with foil, and let it rest for at least 10 minutes.

7 To serve, slice the pork and serve it on top of the vegetables and apples, drizzling the pan juices over the top.

Slow-Roasted Pot Roast with Onions and Carrots

SERVES 10 • PREP: 15 MINUTES, PLUS 10 MINUTES TO REST POT ROAST • COOK: 4 HOURS

ONE POT

1 (4-pound) chuck roast

Kosher salt

Freshly ground
    black pepper

2 tablespoons olive oil

2 onions, cut into wedges

6 carrots, peeled and cut
    into 2-inch lengths

1 cup dry red wine

2 to 3 cups beef broth

3 sprigs thyme

3 sprigs rosemary

Yes, this dish takes most of an afternoon to cook, but the hands-on time is minimal and the end result is so worth the wait. Serve the tender meat and richly flavored vegetables with mashed potatoes, being sure to spoon the pan juices over the potatoes.

1 Preheat the oven to 275°F.

2 Season the roast generously on all sides with salt and pepper.

3 In the Dutch oven, heat the oil over medium-high heat. Add the onions and cook, stirring frequently, until browned, about 5 minutes. Transfer to a plate.

4 Add the carrots to the pot and cook, stirring occasionally, until browned, about 3 minutes. Transfer the carrots to the plate with the onions.

5 Add the roast to the pot and cook, turning occasionally, until browned on all sides, about 5 minutes total. Transfer the roast to the plate with the onions and carrots.

6 Add the wine to the pot and cook, stirring and scraping up any browned bits from the bottom of the pot, about 3 minutes.

7 Return the roast to the pot along with the onions and carrots. Add the broth, thyme, and rosemary. Cover and roast for about 3½ hours, until the roast is very tender and falls apart when tested with a fork. Remove from the oven and let rest at least 10 minutes before slicing or shredding. Remove and discard the thyme and rosemary.

8 Serve hot along with the vegetables.

Braised Lamb Shanks with Persian Spices

SERVES 6 + PREP: 15 MINUTES + COOK: 2 HOURS

ONE POT

4 pounds lamb shanks
(about 4½ pounds)

Kosher salt

Freshly ground
black pepper

2 teaspoons cinnamon

1 teaspoon ground
cardamom

1 teaspoon grated nutmeg

1 teaspoon turmeric

¼ teaspoon crumbled
saffron threads

Juice of 2 limes

½ cup warm water

1 cup vegetable oil

1 large onion,
roughly chopped

Zest of 1 lime

Zest of 1 orange

3 thyme sprigs

2 fresh bay leaves

6 cups chicken broth

Meaty lamb shanks are slow simmered with fragrant spices—cinnamon, nutmeg, cardamom, and turmeric—for an exotically flavored dish that's perfect served over couscous or basmati rice. Lamb often symbolizes renewal and spring, making this a perfect dish for any springtime occasion, including Passover or Easter, or just a quiet spring Sunday.

1 Preheat the oven to 350°F.

2 Season the lamb shanks generously with salt and pepper. In a small bowl, combine the cinnamon, cardamom, nutmeg, and turmeric and rub the mixture into the lamb shanks.

3 In a small bowl, combine the saffron and lime juice with the water.

4 Fill the Dutch oven with about ½ inch of oil and heat it over medium-high heat. Brown the lamb shanks in two batches until browned on all sides, about 5 minutes per batch. As the shanks are browned, transfer them to a plate. >>

5 Drain most of the oil from the Dutch oven, leaving just about 2 tablespoons, and set the pot over medium heat. Add the onion and cook, stirring frequently, until softened and golden, about 8 minutes. Add a bit of salt, the lime zest, orange zest, thyme, bay leaves, and saffron mixture, including the liquid. Return the lamb shanks to the pot, add the broth, and bring to a boil.

6 Remove the pot from the heat, cover, and transfer to the oven. Cook until the meat is very tender, about 1½ hours.

7 Transfer the meat to a serving platter and strain the sauce through a fine-meshed sieve, discarding the solids. Skim off any visible fat, and taste and adjust the seasoning if needed. Remove and discard the thyme sprigs and bay leaves.

8 Serve the meat in chunks, with the juices spooned over.

Korean-Style Braised Short Ribs

SERVES 4 TO 6 · PREP: 10 MINUTES · COOK: 1 HOUR & 40 MINUTES

3 pounds bone-in beef short ribs, cut into ½-inch slices

1 onion, quartered

4 garlic cloves, peeled

1 tart apple, peeled, cored, and cut into quarters

1 (1-inch) piece fresh ginger, peeled

⅓ cup mirin

⅓ cup soy sauce

⅓ cup brown sugar

1 tablespoon sesame oil

1 teaspoon freshly ground black pepper

¼ to ½ teaspoon cayenne pepper

1½ cups water

2 carrots, peeled and cut into 2-inch lengths

1 small radish, cut into 2-inch chunks

Steamed rice (optional)

Meaty short ribs are braised in a flavorful mixture of soy sauce, sugar, sesame oil, garlic, ginger, and a bit of apple for sweetness. This rich and spicy Korean beef dish is delicious served with white rice, or you can serve it with lettuce leaves to wrap the meat in along with fresh herbs (mint, cilantro, and basil) and the spicy-sweet Korean dipping sauce called saam jang.

1 In the Dutch oven, place the short ribs and cover with water. Bring to a boil over high heat and cook for 5 minutes. Drain.

2 In a food processor or blender, combine the onion, garlic, apple, and ginger and process until smooth. Add the mirin and process to combine.

3 Return the ribs to the Dutch oven and pour the onion mixture over the top. Set the pot over low heat and cook, stirring occasionally, for 20 minutes.

4 In a small bowl, combine the soy sauce, brown sugar, sesame oil, black pepper, and cayenne. Add this mixture, along with the water, to the meat and bring to a boil. Reduce the heat to low and simmer, covered, for 40 to 45 minutes.

5 Stir in the carrots and radish and continue to cook, covered, until the meat and vegetables are both very tender, about 30 minutes more.

6 Serve hot with steamed rice (if using).

Short Ribs Braised in Red Wine

SERVES 8 • PREP: 15 MINUTES • COOK: 3 HOURS & 30 MINUTES

ONE POT

5 pounds bone-in beef
    short ribs, cut crosswise
    into 2-inch pieces

Kosher salt

Freshly ground
    black pepper

3 tablespoons vegetable oil

3 onions, diced

3 carrots, peeled and diced

2 celery stalks, diced

3 tablespoons
    all-purpose flour

1 tablespoon tomato paste

1 750-milliliter bottle dry
    red wine (such as
    Cabernet Sauvignon)

10 sprigs flat-leaf parsley

8 sprigs thyme

4 sprigs oregano

2 bay leaves

4 cups beef broth

¼ cup minced flat-leaf
    parsley, for garnish

This is a classic way to cook meaty short ribs—by slow cooking them for hours in a sauce of red wine and aromatic herbs. Serve this dish over mashed potatoes, with Oven-Baked Polenta with Sweet Corn Aioli (page 57), or with crusty bread for sopping up the sauce. Cooking and eating this dish may be the most perfect way to spend a winter Sunday.

1 Preheat the oven to 350°F.

2 Season the meat generously with salt and pepper. In the Dutch oven, heat the oil over medium-high heat. Cook the meat in the pot (brown in batches to avoid crowding the pot), turning occasionally, until browned on all sides, about 8 minutes. As the ribs are browned, transfer them to a plate. Drain off most of the rendered fat from the pot, leaving about 3 tablespoons.

3 Add the onions, carrots, and celery to the Dutch oven and cook, stirring frequently, over medium-high heat until the vegetables are softened and beginning to brown, about 5 minutes.

4 Add the flour and tomato paste and cook, stirring continuously, until the flour is incorporated and the tomato paste darkens, about 3 minutes.

5 Add the wine and the browned short ribs along with any accumulated juices. Bring to a boil, reduce the heat to medium, and let simmer until the liquid is reduced by half, about 30 minutes.

6 Tie the parsley, thyme, oregano, and bay leaves together with a piece of kitchen twine and tuck the bundle into the pot. Add the broth, bring to a boil, and cover. Transfer to the oven and bake until the meat is very tender, about 2½ hours.

7 Remove the ribs from the pot and transfer them to a serving platter. Remove and discard the herb bundle, then strain the sauce through a fine-meshed sieve into a heatproof measuring cup. Skim the visible fat off the surface and taste and adjust the seasoning if needed. Serve hot, drizzled with the sauce and garnished with parsley.

Essential Technique: This dish gets even better the day after it's cooked, so plan ahead for a special dinner. Cook the dish the day before, let it cool to room temperature, cover, and refrigerate. Remove the pot from the refrigerator about 30 minutes before you plan to heat it up so that it can begin to come up to room temperature. Heat in a 350°F oven until bubbling, about 45 minutes.

Beer-Braised Brisket with Ginger

SERVES 8 · PREP: 10 MINUTES, PLUS 10 MINUTES TO REST BRISKET · COOK: 3 HOURS

ONE POT

2 tablespoons vegetable oil

1 (3-pound) beef brisket, trimmed of excess fat and silver skin

Kosher salt

Freshly ground black pepper

1 (2-inch) cinnamon stick

10 whole cloves

4 green cardamom pods, crushed

2 pounds white onions, sliced ½ inch thick (about 3 medium)

1½ tablespoons finely minced garlic

1½ tablespoons grated fresh ginger

1 (22-ounce) lager beer (recommended: Sapporo)

1 tablespoon dark brown sugar

1 cup beef or chicken broth

1 teaspoon apple cider vinegar

I was well into adulthood before I realized brisket wasn't solely Jewish, reserved for holidays like Hanukkah and Passover. Since I'm half Irish (in addition to being half Jewish), it's funny that I didn't realize brisket is also the cut used to make that Irish standby, corned beef. No matter how you slice it, brisket is a cut that's perfect for slow cooking, and this beer-braised version flavored with warm spices like ginger, cinnamon, and cloves is a winner with both sides of my family.

1 Preheat the oven to 325°F.

2 In the Dutch oven, heat the oil over medium-high heat. Season the brisket generously with salt and pepper. Add the brisket to the pot and cook, turning occasionally, until browned on all sides, about 10 minutes. Transfer the browned brisket to a plate.

3 Reduce the heat under the Dutch oven to medium. Toss the cinnamon stick, cloves, and cardamom pods into the pot and cook, stirring, just until they become fragrant, about 1 minute.

4 Add the onions, garlic, and ginger, along with a pinch of salt, and cook, stirring occasionally, until the onions soften and turn golden, about 10 minutes.

5 Deglaze the pot with the beer, stirring and scraping up any browned bits from the bottom of the pot. Stir in the sugar and return the browned brisket to the pot along with any accumulated juices. Add the broth, bring to a boil, and cover. Transfer to the oven and cook until the meat is tender, about 2½ hours.

6 Remove the lid and continue to cook in the oven until the liquid is reduced and thickened and the meat is very tender.

7 Remove the brisket from the pot, transferring it to a carving board. Tent with foil and let it rest for at least 10 minutes.

8 Meanwhile, stir the cider vinegar into the sauce in the pot. If the liquid is very thick, add a bit of water to thin it. Or, if it is thin and watery, set the pot over medium heat and boil until it is reduced to the consistency of gravy. Taste and adjust the seasoning if needed.

9 To serve, slice the brisket thinly across the grain. Serve with the sauce ladled over the top.

Steak Roulades with Blue Cheese, Mushrooms, and Spinach

SERVES 6 • PREP: 10 MINUTES • COOK: 1 HOUR

ONE POT

2 tablespoons vegetable oil, divided

2 sweet onions, such as Vidalia, diced

2 garlic cloves, minced

2 cups mushrooms, thinly sliced

1½ teaspoons kosher salt, divided

1½ teaspoons freshly ground black pepper, divided

2 pounds flank steak, butterflied

5 ounces baby spinach

6 ounces blue cheese, crumbled

2 tablespoons unsalted butter, divided

1 shallot, diced

¾ cup low-salt beef broth

½ cup dry red wine

Steak and blue cheese make a winning combination. Here flavorful flank steak is rolled around a mixture of tangy blue cheese, mushrooms, and spinach and cooked to perfection, then drizzled with a sumptuous red wine reduction. This dish is simple to make but a great dish to serve when you want to impress someone.

1 Preheat the oven to 350°F.

2 In the Dutch oven, heat 1 tablespoon of oil over medium heat. Add the onions, garlic, mushrooms, ½ teaspoon of salt, and ½ teaspoon of pepper and cook, stirring frequently, until the onions and mushrooms are softened and browned, about 20 minutes. Using a slotted spoon, transfer the vegetable mixture to a bowl.

3 Lay the flank steak out flat and spoon the vegetable mixture over the top, spreading it into an even layer covering the meat. Crumble the blue cheese over the vegetables and top with the spinach. Starting with one end of the steak, roll the meat up tightly around the filling. Tie with kitchen twine to hold the roll together. Season the steak all over with the remaining 1 teaspoon of salt and remaining 1 teaspoon of pepper.

4 In the Dutch oven, heat the remaining 1 tablespoon of oil over high heat. Add the steak and cook, turning occasionally, until the steak is browned on all sides, about 5 minutes. Transfer to the oven and bake for about 12 minutes, until the steak is medium-rare. Remove the steak from the pot, transfer it to a cutting board, tent it with foil, and let it rest for 10 minutes.

5 While the steak rests, make the sauce. In the Dutch oven, melt 1 tablespoon of butter over medium-high heat. Add the shallot and cook, stirring, until softened, about 3 minutes.

6 Add the broth and wine to the pot and bring to a boil. Cook until the sauce is reduced to about ½ cup, about 10 minutes. Swirl in the remaining 1 tablespoon of butter.

7 To serve, slice the steak into pinwheels and serve with the sauce spooned over the top.

Essential Technique: To butterfly the steak, place it on a cutting board perpendicular to your body. Placing your nondominant hand on top of the meat, insert the knife along the edge of the steak at the top using your dominant hand and slice through the center of the meat keeping the knife parallel to the cutting board. Cut with the grain, from one side almost to the other, leaving the second edge. Open the steak up like a book. This is simple to do, but you can also ask your butcher to do it for you!

Sweet-and-Sour Stuffed Cabbage

SERVES 6 • PREP: 30 MINUTES • COOK: 1 HOUR & 40 MINUTES

FOR THE SAUCE

2 tablespoons olive oil

1 onion, diced, divided

2 (28-ounce) cans crushed tomatoes

¼ cup red wine vinegar

½ cup (lightly packed) light brown sugar

½ cup raisins

1½ teaspoons kosher salt

¾ teaspoon freshly ground black pepper

FOR THE CABBAGE

1 large head green cabbage

FOR THE FILLING

2½ pounds ground beef

3 large eggs, lightly beaten

1 cup uncooked white rice

1 cup sauerkraut, drained and chopped

1½ teaspoons kosher salt

½ teaspoon freshly ground black pepper

¼ cup minced fresh dill

This is the stuff of Jewish grandmothers—simple and economical ingredients lovingly assembled and tended for hours as they cook and transform into a meal that comforts the soul. Wilted cabbage leaves are stuffed with a savory mixture of ground meat and spices and blanketed in a sweet-and-sour tomato sauce. It just might be the only food more magical than chicken soup.

TO MAKE THE SAUCE

1 In the Dutch oven, heat the oil over medium heat. Add three-quarters of the diced onion (reserve the remaining diced onion for the filling) and cook, stirring frequently, until the onion is softened, about 8 minutes.

2 Stir in the tomatoes, vinegar, brown sugar, raisins, salt, and pepper. Bring the mixture to a boil, reduce the heat to low, and simmer, uncovered, for 30 minutes.

TO MAKE THE CABBAGE

Meanwhile, prepare the cabbage leaves. Bring a large pot of water to a boil. Submerge the whole head of cabbage in the boiling water and cook for about 5 minutes, until the leaves are pliable. Drain in a colander and let cool.

TO MAKE THE FILLING

1 Preheat the oven to 350°F.

2 In a large bowl, combine the ground beef, eggs, rice, sauerkraut, the remaining diced onion, salt, and pepper, and dill.

TO MAKE THE STUFFED CABBAGE

1 When the cabbage leaves are cool enough to handle, peel off about 30 large leaves (reserve any that are small or torn for another purpose). Pat the leaves dry with paper towels and then lay them on a cutting board. Using a sharp paring knife, shave off the thick part of the center rib at the base of each leaf (this will make them easier to roll).

2 Stuff the leaves by placing them flat on the cutting board with the stem end closest to your body, with the edges curling up to form a bowl shape. Place about ⅓ cup of filling at the base of each leaf, about ½ inch from the bottom edge. Fold the base of the leaf up over the filling, covering the filling completely. Fold one of the sides inward, and then continue rolling from the base upward until the leaf is completely rolled around the filling. Tuck the other side of the leaf into the center, creating a neat package. Continue until all of the filling has been used.

3 Transfer most of the sauce from the Dutch oven to a large bowl, leaving about 1 cup of sauce in the pot. Arrange the stuffed cabbage leaves, seam-side down, in a single layer to cover the entire bottom of the pot. Ladle additional sauce over the stuffed cabbage leaves. Continue layering stuffed cabbage leaves and sauce until all of the stuffed leaves are in the pot. Pour any remaining sauce over the top.

4 Cover the pot and bake for 1 hour, until the meat and rice are thoroughly cooked. Serve hot.

Essential Technique: Instead of cooking the head of cabbage in boiling water, you can freeze the cabbage overnight, which will make the leaves pliable. Remove the cabbage from the freezer to defrost about 3 hours before you plan to assemble the rolls.

Pappardelle with Lamb and Porcini Ragu

SERVES 6 • PREP: 15 MINUTES • COOK: 50 MINUTES

1 ounce dried porcini
  mushrooms

2 tablespoons olive oil

2 pounds ground lamb

1½ teaspoons kosher salt

½ teaspoon freshly ground
  black pepper

2 onions, diced

6 garlic cloves, minced

1 large carrot, sliced

4 sprigs rosemary

3 tablespoons minced
  fresh sage

2 cups red wine

1 (28-ounce) can peeled
  whole plum tomatoes

1 pound dried pappardelle
  noodles

2 ounces freshly grated
  Parmesan cheese,
  for garnish

¼ cup minced flat-leaf
  parsley, for garnish

Rich, meaty lamb flavors this simmered tomato sauce, with dried porcinis adding even more depth. Served over wide, flat ribbons of pappardelle pasta, the lush sauce is deeply satisfying. Using ground lamb gives you that slow-simmered flavor without cooking the sauce all day.

1 Bring a large pot of salted water to a boil for the pasta.

2 Place the dried porcini in a heatproof bowl and pour 1 cup of boiling water over them. Set aside.

3 In the Dutch oven, heat the oil over medium-high heat. Add the lamb and cook, stirring, until browned, about 6 minutes. Season with the salt and pepper.

4 Add the onions, reduce the heat to medium, and continue to cook, stirring occasionally, until the onions are golden brown, about 5 minutes more.

5 Stir in the garlic, carrot, rosemary, and sage. Reduce the heat to medium-low and continue to cook, stirring occasionally, until the vegetables soften, about 5 minutes more.

6 Add the wine and bring to a boil over medium heat. Cook, stirring and scraping up any browned bits from the bottom of the pot, until the liquid has reduced by half, about 10 minutes.

7 Meanwhile scoop the porcinis out of the soaking liquid, reserving the liquid, and chop the mushrooms.

8 In the Dutch oven, add the tomatoes, stirring them and breaking them up with a wooden spoon or spatula. Stir in the chopped porcinis and the porcini soaking liquid, being careful to leave the grit that has settled to the bottom of the bowl behind. Simmer until the tomatoes have broken down and the sauce thickens, about 20 minutes more.

9 While the sauce simmers, cook the pasta according to the package directions. Drain.

10 Serve the pasta, topped with the sauce and garnished with Parmesan cheese and parsley.

No-Knead Crusty
French Loaf (page 186)

Chapter Nine

Breads, Rolls & Jams

Cinnamon-Orange Rolls

MAKES ABOUT 12 ROLLS • PREP: 20 MINUTES, PLUS 2 HOURS FOR DOUGH TO RISE • COOK: 30 MINUTES

FOR THE DOUGH

1 envelope active dry yeast

½ cup warm water

½ cup orange juice

¼ cup sugar

⅓ cup unsalted butter, cut into small pieces

1 teaspoon fine sea salt

1 large egg

Zest of 1 orange

3½ to 4 cups all-purpose flour, divided

Oil or butter for coating

FOR THE FILLING

½ cup (1 stick) unsalted butter, at room temperature, plus more for preparing the Dutch oven

¾ cup brown sugar

2 tablespoons cinnamon

FOR THE GLAZE

2 tablespoons unsalted butter, melted

1 cup powdered sugar

1 teaspoon vanilla extract

Zest of 1 orange

2 to 4 tablespoons orange juice

What could be better than a batch of hot cinnamon rolls fresh out of the oven? I really can't think of anything, except maybe a batch of cinnamon-orange rolls hot out of the oven. These are classic cinnamon rolls with a twist—a jolt of orange flavor that comes from both orange juice and zest in both the dough and the glaze.

TO MAKE THE DOUGH

1 In a small bowl, sprinkle the yeast over the warm water. Set aside.

2 In a large bowl or in the bowl of a stand mixer fitted with the dough hook, mix together the orange juice, sugar, butter, salt, egg, and orange zest. Add 2 cups of flour and mix until smooth.

3 Add the yeast mixture and 1½ more cups of the flour, stirring until the dough comes together and is easy to handle. If the dough is too sticky, add additional flour, a little at a time, until the dough is tacky but smooth enough to handle.

4 Turn the dough out onto a lightly floured surface and knead until smooth, 5 to 10 minutes (if using a stand mixer, you can knead it in the bowl with the dough hook).

5 Put the dough in a large bowl that has been coated with oil or butter, cover, and set in a warm spot on your countertop to rise until doubled in size, about 1 to 1½ hours.

TO FILL THE DOUGH

1 Transfer the dough to a lightly floured surface, punch it down, and roll it out into a large rectangle (about 15 by 9 inches). Spread the butter evenly over the dough, and then sprinkle evenly with the brown sugar and cinnamon.

2 Starting with one of the long sides, roll the dough up as tightly as possible into a log. Using a serrated knife, cut the log into 12 slices.

3 Lightly coat the inside of the Dutch oven with butter.

4 Arrange the slices, cut sides up, in a single layer, in the prepared Dutch oven. Set in a warm spot on your counter-top to rise until doubled in size, about 45 minutes.

5 Preheat the oven to 350°F.

6 Bake the rolls, uncovered, for 25 to 30 minutes, until golden brown on top.

TO MAKE THE GLAZE

1 While the rolls are baking, in a medium bowl, whisk together the melted butter, powdered sugar, vanilla, and orange zest. Add the orange juice 1 tablespoon at a time until the glaze reaches the desired consistency.

2 Remove the rolls from the oven and let cool, about 15 minutes. Drizzle the glaze over the top. Serve warm or at room temperature.

Essential Technique: Make these rolls overnight so you can have fresh, hot rolls in the morning. Follow the recipe through arranging the slices in the Dutch oven, but instead of letting the dough rise on the countertop, cover the pot and let it rise in the refrigerator overnight. In the morning, remove the pot from the refrigerator and let the dough rise in a warm spot on the counter-top for about 1 hour. Bake as directed.

Cherry and Dark Chocolate Scones

MAKES 10 TO 12 SCONES • PREP: 10 MINUTES • COOK: 25 MINUTES

Butter for preparing
the Dutch oven

2 cups all-purpose flour

4 teaspoons baking powder

½ teaspoon fine sea salt

¼ cup sugar, plus additional
for sprinkling (optional)

½ cup (1 stick) unsalted
butter, very cold and cut
into small pieces

2 large eggs, lightly beaten

¾ cup whole milk, plus
2 tablespoons

2 tablespoons heavy cream

½ cup coarsely chopped
dried cherries

½ cup semisweet
chocolate chips

Seasonal Swap: Dried
cherries and chocolate
chips are available
any time of year, but
if you'd like to make a
seasonal version with
fresh fruit, substitute
1 cup of pears, apples,
peaches, apricots,
nectarines, strawber-
ries, blueberries, or
blackberries for both
the cherries and choc-
olate chips.

These simple scones bake perfectly nestled inside the piping hot walls of the Dutch oven. They come out delightfully tender with a bit of crunch on the outside. Studded with dried cherries and dark chocolate, they make a slightly decadent afternoon snack. If you're looking for something a bit more health conscious, you could substitute chopped almonds or walnuts for the chocolate chips.

1 Preheat the oven to 400°F and coat the inside of the Dutch oven with butter.

2 In a large bowl, whisk together the flour, baking powder, salt, and sugar. Mix the cold butter into the flour mixture with a pastry cutter or your fingertips, until the mixture resembles fine bread crumbs.

3 In a small bowl, combine the eggs, ¾ cup of milk, and the cream. Stir in the dried cherries and chocolate chips. Add the egg mixture to the flour mixture and mix until a dough forms.

4 Separate the dough into 10 to 12 balls of equal size. Nestle the balls of dough in the prepared Dutch oven and brush the tops with the remaining 2 tablespoons of milk. Sprinkle with a bit of sugar (if using). Bake, uncovered, for 20 to 25 minutes, until golden brown. If the tops begin to brown too quickly, place the lid on the Dutch oven for the remainder of the cooking time.

Honey-Jalapeño Cornbread

SERVES 8 • PREP: 10 MINUTES • COOK: 30 MINUTES

¾ cup unsalted butter, divided

1½ cups cornmeal

1½ cups all-purpose flour

1½ tablespoons baking powder

1½ teaspoons salt

1½ cups whole milk

¾ cup honey

2 large eggs

1 to 2 jalapeño chiles, seeded and finely chopped

Essential Technique: Once you mix together the wet and dry ingredients, stir just enough to combine the two completely. Overmixing will result in a dry cornbread.

This cornbread is perfectly moist, sweet, and spicy. Cooking it in the Dutch oven gives it a delightfully crisp outer crust. In the summertime, when fresh corn is at its peak, add the kernels from two or three ears of corn to make it even more special. Serve this alongside bowls of chili or just slather it with butter and eat it by itself.

1 Preheat the oven to 400°F.

2 Melt ½ cup of butter in the microwave.

3 In a large bowl, whisk together the cornmeal, flour, baking powder, and salt.

4 In a medium bowl, whisk together the milk, honey, and eggs. Add the egg mixture to the dry ingredients and stir until just combined.

5 Stir in the jalapeño and the melted butter.

6 In the Dutch oven, melt the remaining ¼ cup of butter over medium-high heat. Stir or swirl the butter around in the pot to coat, until it melts completely.

7 Pour the batter into the Dutch oven and transfer to the oven. Bake for 25 to 30 minutes, until the edges are browned and a tester inserted into the center comes out clean.

8 Let the cornbread cool in the pot for about 10 minutes, and then invert it onto a serving platter. Serve warm or at room temperature, cut into wedges.

Fluffy Buttermilk Biscuits

MAKES 10 TO 12 BISCUITS • PREP: 10 MINUTES • COOK: 20 MINUTES

3 cups all-purpose flour

1 tablespoon baking powder

3 tablespoons sugar

½ teaspoon fine sea salt

½ teaspoon baking soda

½ cup (1 stick) frozen unsalted butter

1 cup buttermilk

2 tablespoons heavy cream

These slightly sweet, buttery biscuits make a fantastic base for a ham sandwich, but they're just as good spread with butter and jam or honey. The key to making them light and fluffy is to start with frozen butter and mix very gently.

1 Preheat the oven to 425°F.

2 In a large bowl, whisk together the flour, baking powder, sugar, salt, and baking soda.

3 Using the large holes of a box grater, grate the frozen butter into the dry ingredients. Toss until the bits of butter are coated with the flour mixture and then gently stir in the buttermilk until the dough comes together.

4 Turn the dough out onto a lightly floured cutting board and knead for about 30 seconds, just until the dough holds together.

5 Form the dough into a disc and then roll it out, using a floured rolling pin, into an even thickness, about ¾ of an inch. Use a 3-inch round cookie or biscuit cutter, or a juice glass, to cut the dough into rounds.

6 Place the circles in the Dutch oven in a single layer and brush the cream over the tops. Bake, uncovered, for 15 to 20 minutes, until the biscuits are golden brown.

Bacon, Cheddar, and Chive Pull-Apart Bread

SERVES 8 • PREP: 10 MINUTES, PLUS 30 MINUTES TO REST DOUGH • COOK: 15 MINUTES

Butter for preparing
the Dutch oven

2 cups all-purpose flour,
plus more for dusting

1 tablespoon baking powder

1 tablespoon sugar

1 teaspoon fine sea salt

1 teaspoon baking soda

5 tablespoons unsalted
butter, frozen

1 cup whole milk, plus
2 tablespoons

1 large egg

6 strips bacon, cooked
and crumbled

¾ cup shredded
Cheddar cheese

¼ cup minced chives

Every bite of this decadent bread is loaded with bacon, cheese, and chives, making it a satisfying snack or appetizer on its own.

1 Preheat the oven to 425°F and coat the inside of the Dutch oven with butter.

2 In a large bowl, whisk together the flour, baking powder, sugar, salt, and baking soda.

3 Using the large holes of a box grater, grate the frozen butter into the dry ingredients. Toss until the shreds of butter are coated with the flour mixture and then gently stir in 1 cup of milk until the dough comes together in a rough ball.

4 Turn the dough out onto a floured cutting board and pat it into an even rectangle, about 1 inch thick. Fold the rectangle over and pat it down again to 1 inch thick. Repeat folding and patting once more. Cover with a clean dish towel and let it rest for 30 minutes.

5 Gently pat out the dough once more into a rectangle that is roughly 10 inches by 6 inches. Using a sharp knife, cut the dough into 2-inch squares.

6 In a large bowl, whisk together the egg and the remaining 2 tablespoons of milk. Add the biscuit pieces and stir gently to coat. Fold in the bacon, Cheddar cheese, and chives. Transfer the mixture to the prepared Dutch oven and bake, uncovered, for 12 to 15 minutes, until golden brown.

7 To serve, transfer to a serving platter and let guests pull off chunks.

No-Knead Crusty French Loaf

MAKES A 1¼-POUND LOAF • PREP: 15 MINUTES, PLUS 14 TO 26 HOURS TO RISE • COOK: 1 HOUR

¾ teaspoon active dry yeast

½ teaspoon sugar

1⅓ cups water, plus
more as needed

3 cups bread flour,
plus additional flour
(all-purpose is fine)
for dusting

1 teaspoon fine sea salt

2 tablespoons olive oil

No-knead breads have been taking the home-baking world by storm for a few years now. This method starts with a no-knead dough that is baked in a preheated Dutch oven, which traps the steam escaping from the dough as it cooks, giving the bread a delectably crunchy outer crust. In terms of active time, this method involves only about 15 hands-on minutes, but the complete recipe takes up to 27 hours from start to finish, so plan accordingly.

1 In a small bowl, sprinkle the yeast and sugar over the water. Stir gently to mix. Let sit for about 10 minutes, until the mixture is frothy.

2 Meanwhile, in a large bowl, combine the bread flour and salt.

3 Once the yeast mixture develops a layer of foam on top, give the mixture a quick stir and then add it to the bread flour along with the olive oil, stirring with a wooden spoon at first and then with your hands, until the dough comes together into a sticky ball. If necessary, add a bit more water, 1 tablespoon at a time and kneading after each addition, until the dough holds together.

4 Cover the bowl and let it stand on your countertop to rise for at least 12 hours and up to 24 hours. The dough will rise significantly and become dry and crusty on top.

5 Dust a clean dish towel lightly with flour and then turn the dough out onto it, scraping it out of the bowl if necessary. Tuck the crusty top of the dough inside, and reshape the ball into a slightly flattened ball. Wrap the dough up in the towel and set on the countertop to rise for an additional 2 hours.

6 Preheat the oven to 475°F with the covered Dutch oven inside.

7 When ready to bake, remove the heated Dutch oven from the oven. Take off the lid, turn the dough off the towel and into the pot, cover again, and bake for 30 minutes. Remove the lid and continue baking for 15 to 30 minutes more, until the crust is a deep, golden brown.

8 Remove the pot from the oven, carefully remove the bread from the pot (silicone spatulas and oven mitts work well here), and let the bread cool on a wire rack for at least 1 hour before slicing. Serve at room temperature.

Essential Technique: It is best to use bread flour for this recipe since it has a higher protein content than all-purpose or other flours. The higher protein contributes to the development of gluten, which gives the bread its prized chewiness and helps the bread rise as much as possible.

Multigrain Bread with Cranberries and Walnuts

MAKES A 1 ¼ POUND LOAF • PREP: 15 MINUTES, PLUS 14 TO 26 HOURS TO RISE • COOK: 1 HOUR

¾ teaspoon active dry yeast

½ teaspoon sugar

1 ⅓ cups water, plus
    more as needed

1 cup bread flour

1 cup whole-wheat flour

1 cup rolled oats

1 teaspoon fine sea salt

1 cup dried cranberries

1 cup chopped walnuts

This multigrain bread is also a no-knead bread, but this one combines bread flour with whole-wheat flour and oats for a heartier, denser loaf. Cranberries and walnuts add texture and flavor. This makes great bread for toasting and slathering with butter or jam, and it also makes great sandwich bread, especially for grilled cheese sandwiches.

1 In a small bowl, sprinkle the yeast and sugar over the water. Stir gently to mix. Let sit for about 10 minutes, until the mixture is frothy.

2 Meanwhile, in a large bowl, combine the bread flour, whole-wheat flour, oats, and salt.

3 Once the yeast mixture develops a layer of foam on top, give the mixture a quick stir and then add it to the bread flour mixture, stirring with a wooden spoon at first and then with your hands, until the dough comes together into a sticky ball.

4 Add the cranberries and walnuts and mix to incorporate. If necessary, add a bit more water, 1 tablespoon at a time, kneading after each addition, until the dough holds together.

5 Cover the bowl and let stand on your countertop to rise for at least 12 hours and up to 24 hours. The dough will rise significantly and become dry and crusty on top.

6 Dust a clean dish towel lightly with flour and then turn the dough out onto it, scraping it out of the bowl if necessary. Tuck the crusty top of the dough inside and reshape the ball into a slightly flattened ball. Wrap the dough up in the towel and set on the countertop to rise for an additional 2 hours.

7 Preheat the oven to 475°F with the covered Dutch oven inside.

8 When ready to bake, remove the heated Dutch oven from the oven. Take off the lid, turn the dough off the towel and into the pot, cover again, and bake for 30 minutes. Remove the lid and continue baking for 20 to 40 minutes more, until the crust is a deep, golden brown.

9 Remove the pot from the oven, carefully remove the bread from the pot (silicone spatulas and oven mitts work well here), and let the bread cool on a wire rack for at least 1 hour before slicing. Serve at room temperature.

Savory Plum and Onion Jam with Thyme

MAKES ABOUT 1 ½ CUPS • PREP: 10 MINUTES • COOK: 1 HOUR

2 tablespoons olive oil

1 onion, diced

1 ½ cups pitted and diced ripe plums

1 tablespoon minced fresh thyme

½ cup red wine

¼ cup water

¼ cup sugar

½ teaspoon kosher salt

The high, even, and sustained heat of the cast iron does a wonderful job of boiling out the water, reducing the juices, and caramelizing the sugars of this sweet, savory plum and onion jam. Spread it on Fluffy Buttermilk Biscuits (page 182) or No-Knead Crusty French Loaf (page 186), or enjoy it as an accompaniment to roast pork or sharp cheeses.

1 In the Dutch oven, heat the oil over medium-high heat. Add the onion and cook, stirring frequently, until softened, about 5 minutes.

2 Add the plums and cook a few minutes more, until the fruit begins to break down.

3 Stir in the thyme, wine, water, sugar, and salt and bring to a boil. Reduce the heat to medium-low and simmer, stirring occasionally, until the mixture is thick and syrupy, about 50 to 60 minutes.

4 Serve warm or at room temperature.

Seasonal Swap: When plums aren't in season, you can substitute 1 cup diced pitted prunes for the fresh plums.

Strawberry-Rhubarb Jam

MAKES ABOUT 3 CUPS • PREP: 10 MINUTES • COOK: 30 MINUTES

2 cups crushed fresh
strawberries

1 cup chopped fresh
rhubarb

2 tablespoons freshly
squeezed lemon juice

2¼ cups sugar

*Rhubarb adds a tart edge to balance out the sweet-
ness of strawberries in this delightful pectin-free jam.
Serve it spread on buttermilk biscuits, dolloped onto
pancakes or waffles, stirred into plain yogurt, or in a
nut butter sandwich. If you can't find fresh rhubarb, you
can substitute frozen (defrost it before adding to the
pot). Make a large batch and can it if you like, or store
it, covered, in the refrigerator for up to two weeks.*

1 In the Dutch oven, combine the strawberries, rhubarb,
and lemon juice and bring to a boil, stirring frequently.
Stir in the sugar and return to a vigorous boil. Cook, stirring nearly continuously, until the sugar is fully dissolved
and the mixture thickens, 25 to 30 minutes.

2 Remove from the heat and skim any foam off the top,
and then transfer the mixture to a heatproof bowl or jar.
Let cool to room temperature before storing or serving.

Essential Technique: Use a candy or deep-fry
thermometer to monitor the temperature of the jam
as it cooks. The jam needs to reach 220°F in order to set.

Chocolate
Clafouti with
Fresh Raspberries
(page 203)

Chapter Ten

Desserts

Caramelized Pear Upside-Down Cake

SERVES 8 · PREP: 15 MINUTES · COOK: 35 MINUTES

½ cup (1 stick) unsalted butter, at room temperature, divided

½ cup brown sugar

2 ripe but firm Bosc pears, peeled, cored, and thinly sliced

1½ cups all-purpose flour

1 teaspoon baking powder

½ teaspoon baking soda

¼ teaspoon salt

½ cup sugar

2 large eggs

1 teaspoon vanilla extract

½ cup plus 3 tablespoons buttermilk

Whipped cream or crème fraîche (optional)

Whether you are using a cast iron skillet or a Dutch oven, start this recipe by melting butter and sugar in the pan or pot, then artfully arrange sliced fruit on top. Pour the cake batter over. Because the sugar and fruit are in direct contact with the hot cast iron bottom of the pot, they caramelize to perfection, creating a visually stunning topping when the cake is inverted onto a serving platter.

1 Preheat the oven to 350°F.

2 In the Dutch oven, melt 2 tablespoons of butter over medium-high heat. Add the brown sugar and stir to combine. Arrange the pear slices on top of the butter and sugar mixture in the pot. Remove the pot from the heat.

3 In a medium bowl, whisk together the flour, baking powder, baking soda, and salt.

4 In a large bowl using an electric mixer or in a stand mixer, cream together the remaining 6 tablespoons of butter and the sugar at medium-high speed for about 3 minutes, until well combined.

5 Add the eggs one at a time, beating after each addition to incorporate. Add the vanilla.

6 With the mixer set on low speed, add the flour mixture and the buttermilk in three alternating batches and mix to combine.

7 Spoon the batter over the pears in the Dutch oven, spreading the batter out carefully with a spatula or the back of a spoon into an even layer. Bake for 25 to 30 minutes, until a tester inserted into the center comes out with only a few crumbs attached.

8 To serve, you can invert the cake onto a serving platter, or simply slice it into wedges and serve it from the Dutch oven. Serve warm or at room temperature with a dollop of whipped cream or crème fraîche (if using).

Lemon Pudding Cakes in Mini Cocottes

SERVES 4 • PREP: 15 MINUTES • COOK: 30 MINUTES

Zest of 3 lemons, divided

¼ cup freshly squeezed lemon juice

1 tablespoon freshly squeezed orange juice

1½ teaspoons grated fresh ginger

3 egg yolks, 2 of the whites reserved

1 cup whole milk

½ teaspoon vanilla extract

1 cup sugar, divided

⅛ teaspoon salt

¼ cup all-purpose flour

The first time I made a pudding cake, I must have been about 12 years old, and I seriously thought some sort of dark magic was at play. How could a handful of normal cake ingredients turn into a perfectly layered masterpiece of cake and pudding? These mini tart–sweet lemon pudding cakes make a truly magical end to a special meal.

1 Preheat the oven to 350°F and set a kettle with 4 cups of water to boil.

2 In a large bowl, whisk together the zest of 2 of the lemons with the lemon juice, orange juice, ginger, and egg yolks. Whisking constantly, add the milk and vanilla and whisk until combined.

3 Add ½ cup of sugar, the salt, and the flour and continue whisking until smooth.

4 In a large bowl using an electric mixer or in a stand mixer, whip the egg whites to soft peaks. Whisk about one-fourth of the whipped whites into the batter and then gently fold in the remaining whipped whites just until incorporated.

5 Place 10- or 12-ounce mini cocottes into a baking dish or roasting pan and spoon the batter into them, dividing evenly. Pour the boiling water into the dish, being careful not to splash any into the batter, until it reaches about halfway up the sides of the cocottes.

6 Carefully transfer the baking dish or roasting pan into the oven. Bake for 30 minutes, until nicely puffed and golden brown on top.

7 Transfer the cocottes to a wire rack and let cool for 10 minutes. Serve warm, garnished with the remaining lemon zest and the remaining ½ cup of sugar.

Blackberry and Peach Cobbler

SERVES 6 TO 8 • PREP: 10 MINUTES • COOK: 45 MINUTES

Butter for preparing the
  Dutch oven

2 tablespoons cornstarch

1½ cups sugar, plus
  1 teaspoon

6 peaches (about 2 pounds),
  peeled, pitted, and cut
  into wedges

5 cups (about 1¼ pounds)
  blackberries

½ teaspoon lemon zest

3 cups all-purpose flour

1 tablespoon baking powder

1 teaspoon fine sea salt

1 cup (2 sticks) cold
  unsalted butter, cut
  into small pieces

1 cup plus 3 tablespoons
  whole milk

¼ teaspoon lemon zest

Vanilla ice cream, for serving

In the summertime when the blackberry bushes explode with dark, juicy fruit, this simple cobbler is always on the menu. It's a simple way to take advantage of all that ripe summer fruit. The flaky crust is easy to whip up, and there's nothing better to serve under a scoop of cold, creamy vanilla ice cream.

1 Preheat the oven to 425°F and coat the Dutch oven with butter.

2 In the prepared Dutch oven, combine the cornstarch and 1½ cups of sugar. Add the peaches, blackberries, and lemon zest and toss to mix. Bake for 15 minutes, until the mixture is hot and bubbling.

3 Meanwhile, in a large bowl, whisk together the flour, baking powder, and salt. Add the butter and blend with your fingertips until the mixture resembles fine bread crumbs. Gently stir in the milk until well combined.

4 Remove the Dutch oven from the oven and drop the batter on top of the fruit by the heaping tablespoonful. Sprinkle the remaining 1 teaspoon of sugar over the batter. Return to the oven and continue to bake, uncovered, for about 30 minutes, until the crust is golden brown.

5 Serve hot with vanilla ice cream.

Seasonal Swap: You can make this simple cobbler with many different fruit combinations. Instead of peaches, try plums, nectarines, apricots, cherries, apples, or pears. Instead of blackberries, use raspberries, strawberries, or blueberries.

Chocolate Brioche Bread Pudding

SERVES 10 • PREP: 15 MINUTES, PLUS 1 HOUR TO SOAK • COOK: 1 HOUR

Butter for preparing
    the Dutch oven

4½ cups half-and-half

¾ cup sugar

¼ teaspoon fine sea salt

16 ounces bittersweet or
    semisweet chocolate,
    chopped

9 large eggs

2 teaspoons vanilla extract

6 cups (about 1 pound)
    cubed day-old brioche

¼ cup unsalted butter, cut
    into small pieces

This rich, chocolatey bread pudding is truly decadent. Serve it when you really want to wow someone. Serve it dolloped with unsweetened or lightly sweetened whipped cream or crème fraîche and fresh berries.

1 Coat the inside of the Dutch oven generously with butter.

2 In a large saucepan, heat the half-and-half, sugar, and salt over medium heat, stirring frequently, until the sugar dissolves and the mixture is very hot (do not boil).

3 Remove the saucepan from the heat and add the chopped chocolate. Let the chocolate sit in the hot mixture for a couple of minutes to soften, and then whisk until smooth.

4 In a large bowl, beat the eggs and then slowly add the chocolate mixture, whisking constantly, until well combined. Add the vanilla and whisk to incorporate.

5 In the prepared Dutch oven, place the bread cubes and pour the chocolate mixture over the top. Let stand at room temperature, submerging the bread cubes every once in a while, for 1 hour.

6 Preheat the oven to 325°F.

7 Scatter the pieces of butter over the top of the bread pudding. Bake for 50 to 60 minutes, until the edge is mostly set. The center will set further as the dish cools.

8 Transfer to a cooling rack and let cool for about 15 minutes before serving. Serve warm.

Espresso Pound Cake in Mini Cocottes

SERVES 2 TO 4 • PREP: 15 MINUTES • COOK: 40 MINUTES

Butter for preparing the
   mini cocottes

1½ cups sifted cake flour

¼ teaspoon baking soda

¼ teaspoon baking powder

¼ teaspoon fine sea salt

½ cup sour cream

1 tablespoon instant
   espresso powder

1 teaspoon vanilla extract

½ cup (1 stick) unsalted
   butter, at room
   temperature

1¼ cups sugar

3 large eggs

My grandmother used to say she had to have "a little something sweet" with her coffee, by which she usually meant a slice of cake. This rich pound cake is lightly flavored with espresso powder, making it the perfect accompaniment to a cup of coffee. Add a simple vanilla glaze or top it with a scoop of vanilla ice cream if you need even more sweetness.

1 Preheat the oven to 325°F and coat two 12-ounce mini cocottes with butter.

2 In a medium bowl, combine the flour, baking soda, baking powder, and salt.

3 In a small bowl, stir together the sour cream, espresso powder, and vanilla, until the powder dissolves and is well incorporated.

4 In a large bowl using an electric mixer or in the bowl of a stand mixer, cream together the butter and sugar until the mixture is fluffy and light. >>

5 Add the eggs one at a time, beating after each addition to incorporate.

6 Add half of the flour mixture to the butter and egg mixture and beat to combine. Add the sour cream mixture and beat to incorporate. Add the remaining flour mixture and beat until combined. Transfer the batter to the prepared mini cocottes.

7 Bake, uncovered, in the preheated oven for about 40 minutes, until a toothpick inserted into the center comes out clean.

8 Remove from the oven and cool slightly on a wire rack. Invert the cakes out of the cocottes and cut into wedges to serve.

Did You Know? Cake flour has less protein than all-purpose flour (8 percent for cake flour versus 10 to 11 percent for all-purpose). Protein turns to gluten, and gluten is what gives baked goods their chewiness. Lower-protein cake flour is used to make tender-crumbed cakes, while all-purpose flour is used when you want a denser, chewier product.

Chocolate Clafouti with Fresh Raspberries

SERVES 6 · PREP: 10 MINUTES, PLUS 20 MINUTES TO COOL · COOK: 35 MINUTES

Butter for preparing
the Dutch oven

2¾ cups raspberries,
divided

1 tablespoon sugar

1 cup whole milk

¼ cup unsalted
butter, melted

3 large eggs

½ cup (packed) brown sugar

⅓ cup all-purpose flour

2 tablespoons unsweetened
cocoa powder

¼ teaspoon fine sea salt

3 ounces dark chocolate,
coarsely chopped

Clafouti is a classic French dessert that falls somewhere between a pancake and a baked custard. It is lightly browned around the edges, with a moist, creamy center. Adding chocolate to the batter is a delicious departure from tradition, but the rich flavor is perfect with fresh raspberries.

1 Preheat the oven to 400°F and coat the bottom and sides of the Dutch oven with butter.

2 In a medium bowl, toss together 2 cups of raspberries with the sugar.

3 In a blender or food processor, combine the milk, melted butter, eggs, brown sugar, flour, cocoa, and salt and process until smooth.

4 Put the sugared raspberries in the prepared Dutch oven, distributing them evenly across the bottom of the pot. Pour the batter over the berries. Sprinkle the chopped chocolate over the top and stir it into the batter (without disturbing the berries on the bottom).

5 Bake in the preheated oven until the top puffs and firms up, about 35 minutes. Remove from the oven and let cool for 20 minutes.

6 Serve warm, with the remaining ¾ cup of raspberries scattered on top.

Buttermilk Beignets with Maple Glaze

MAKES 48 BEIGNETS • PREP: 15 MINUTES, PLUS 1 HOUR TO RISE • COOK: 20 MINUTES

¾ cup whole milk

1½ cups buttermilk

4 teaspoons active
   dry yeast

2½ tablespoons sugar

3½ cups bread flour,
   plus extra for flouring
   the work surface

½ teaspoon baking soda

¼ teaspoon fine sea salt

1½ cups powdered sugar

¼ cup maple syrup

Vegetable oil, for frying

Beignets *is really just a fancy word for donuts—delicious fried dough with a sweet topping. Traditionally, they are served buried under a mountain of powdered sugar, which is delicious, but this simple maple glaze is an extra-special topping for the crispy fritters.*

1 In a small saucepan over medium-high heat, warm the milk just until bubbles begin to appear around the edges (do not boil).

2 Remove the pot from the heat and stir in the buttermilk. Transfer the mixture to a large bowl or the bowl of a stand mixer and whisk in the yeast and sugar. Let sit for 5 minutes. Add the flour, baking soda, and salt and mix using a handheld electric mixer or a stand mixer fitted with the dough hook for about 4 minutes, until combined.

3 Increase the speed of the mixer to medium and mix until the dough comes together in a loose ball, about 2 minutes more. The dough should still be sticky. Cover the bowl and let rise in a warm spot on your countertop for 1 hour.

4 While the dough is rising, make the glaze. In a medium bowl, stir together the powdered sugar and maple syrup. Set a wire rack over a baking sheet (to catch the drips after you glaze the beignets).

5 Fill the Dutch oven with about 3 inches of oil and heat over high heat for about 15 minutes, until the oil registers 375°F on a deep-fry thermometer. Line a plate with paper towels.

6 Turn the dough out onto a lightly floured work surface and flatten gently with your hands. Sprinkle the top of the dough with flour and fold it in half. Gently form it into a 8-by-10-inch rectangle with your hands. Sprinkle with a bit more flour and then cut it into about 48 1½-inch squares.

7 Drop the dough squares into the hot oil, cooking a few at a time to avoid crowding the pot and turning often, until they puff up and turn golden brown, about 1 minute.

8 Using a slotted spoon or spider, transfer the beignets to the prepared plate. Drop a second batch of dough into the oil, and as they cook, dunk the first batch in the glaze, turning to coat, and then transfer them to the wire rack to cool. Repeat until all of the dough squares have been cooked and glazed.

Coconut-Rice Pudding

SERVES 8 • PREP: 5 MINUTES • COOK: 40 MINUTES

4½ cups cooked rice

2 (14-ounce) cans
coconut milk

1 cup sugar

½ teaspoon kosher salt

1 teaspoon vanilla extract

A version of this simple coconut milk and rice pudding is often served in Thailand topped with slices of fresh, ripe mango. It's a great way to use up leftover rice (make sure it is unsalted; if your rice has salt added, omit the salt in the recipe) and is an easy dessert to whip up using pantry staples. I like to top it with toasted coconut shavings for a bit of textural contrast.

In the Dutch oven, combine the rice, coconut milk, sugar, and salt and bring to a simmer over medium-high heat. Cook, stirring frequently, until the mixture thickens, 35 to 40 minutes. Stir in the vanilla and serve warm.

Butterscotch Custard in Mini Cocottes

SERVES 4 • PREP: 10 MINUTES, PLUS 2 HOURS TO CHILL • COOK: 55 MINUTES

3 tablespoons
   unsalted butter

1 ½ cups (packed) dark
   brown sugar

¾ teaspoon kosher salt

1 ½ cups heavy cream

1 ¼ cups whole milk

6 egg yolks

1 tablespoon vanilla extract

Essential Technique: Are you wondering what to do with the whites that came along with the 6 yolks used in this recipe? Save them, in a covered container, in the refrigerator for a few days or freeze them indefinitely (you can put one each in ice cube tray wells or put several in a freezer-safe resealable bag). Later you can add them to omelets, soufflés, or meringue.

Butterscotch pudding is an old-school, homey dessert. This refined custard, thickened with egg yolks instead of cornstarch, is just as delicious, as simple to prepare, and just a step or two more elegant than its pudding counterpart.

1 Preheat the oven to 325°F and set a kettle of 4 cups of water to boil.

2 In a medium saucepan, melt the butter over medium heat and then stir in the sugar and salt until well combined. Add the cream and milk and continue heating until small bubbles just begin to appear around the edges (do not boil). Remove the pan from the heat.

3 In a medium bowl, add the egg yolks and, whisking constantly, add the warm sugar-milk mixture until combined. Stir in the vanilla. Strain the mixture through a fine-meshed sieve to ensure a smooth texture.

4 Place four 10- or 12-ounce mini cocottes in a baking dish and ladle the mixture into them, dividing evenly. Pour boiling water into the baking dish, being careful not to splash any into the custard, until the water reaches about halfway up the sides of the cocottes.

5 Lightly cover the baking dish with a large sheet of aluminum foil, leaving it loose enough that there is some air flow in and out. Bake the custard for about 45 minutes, turning the pan halfway through for even cooking, until the custard is mostly set (it will set a bit more as it cools).

6 Transfer to the refrigerator and chill for at least 2 hours before serving. Serve chilled.

Pecan-Caramel Monkey Bread

SERVES 6 • PREP: 25 MINUTES, PLUS 1 HOUR & 45 MINUTES TO RISE • COOK: 40 MINUTES

FOR THE DOUGH

2 tablespoons unsalted
    butter, melted, plus
    additional to coat the
    bowl and Dutch oven

1 cup milk, warmed
    to 115°F

⅓ cup water, warmed
    to 115°F

¼ cup sugar

1 packet (2¼ teaspoons)
    rapid-rise yeast

3¼ cups all-purpose flour,
    plus extra for dusting

2 teaspoons fine sea salt

FOR THE CARAMEL-PECAN TOPPING

¾ cup unsalted butter

1½ cups (packed)
    brown sugar

¾ cup chopped,
    toasted pecans

For this delightful dessert, sweet, buttery biscuit dough is rolled into balls, coated with a caramel-pecan coating, and then stacked in the Dutch oven and baked to ooey-gooey perfection. This is a dessert that is fun to make, and even more fun to eat.

Preheat the oven to 175°F. Once it gets to temperature, turn it off.

TO MAKE THE DOUGH

1 In a small bowl, whisk together the butter, milk, water, sugar, and yeast. Set aside.

2 In a large bowl, stir the flour and salt together. Add the milk mixture and stir until the dough comes together into a ball.

3 Transfer the ball to a lightly floured work surface and knead it with your hands until smooth, about 10 minutes.

4 Place the dough ball into a bowl coated with a bit of melted butter, turning it to coat all over with butter. Cover the bowl and set it in the warm oven (with the heat turned off) to rise until it has doubled in size, about 1 hour.

5 Once the dough has risen, place it on a lightly floured work surface and pat it out or use a rolling pin to roll it out into a square roughly 8 inches by 8 inches. Cut the dough into 1-inch squares (you should end up with 64 squares). Roll each dough square into a ball.

TO MAKE THE CARAMEL-PECAN TOPPING

1 In a small saucepan, melt the butter over medium heat. Add the brown sugar and cook, stirring constantly, until the sugar is dissolved, about 3 minutes.

2 Remove from the heat and stir in the pecans.

TO ASSEMBLE THE BREAD

1 Coat the Dutch oven with melted butter and cover the bottom of the pot with a layer of dough balls (they should be close but not pressed up against one another; you want the caramel mixture to run in between the balls). Pour some of the caramel mixture over the dough balls and then place another layer of dough balls on top. Continue layering dough balls and the caramel mixture until both have been used up.

2 Once you have used up all of the dough balls, cover the Dutch oven and let it rise in the warm oven another 45 minutes (the dough balls should expand to completely fill the diameter of the Dutch oven).

3 Remove the Dutch oven from the oven and preheat the oven to 350°F.

4 Bake the monkey bread, uncovered, for about 40 minutes, until browned and cooked through. Carefully invert the monkey bread onto a serving platter, or use heatproof spatulas to transfer it. Serve warm or at room temperature.

Essential technique: If you have a stand mixer, you can save yourself a bit of effort by mixing and kneading the dough in it. Use the dough hook, and oil it before you begin kneading so that the dough doesn't stick to and climb the hook as you mix.

The Dirty Dozen & Clean Fifteen

A nonprofit and environmental watchdog organization called Environmental Working Group (EWG) looks at data supplied by the US Department of Agriculture (USDA) and the Food and Drug Administration (FDA) about pesticide residues and compiles a list each year of the best and worst pesticide loads found in commercial crops. You can refer to the Dirty Dozen list to know which fruits and vegetables you should always buy organic. The Clean Fifteen list lets you know which produce is considered safe enough when grown conventionally to allow you to skip the organics. This does not mean that the Clean Fifteen produce is pesticide-free, though, so wash these fruits and vegetables thoroughly.

These lists change every year, so make sure you look up the most recent before you fill your shopping cart. You'll find the most recent lists as well as a guide to pesticides in produce at EWG.ORG/FOODNEWS.

2016 Dirty Dozen

Apples	Nectarines	Sweet bell peppers	*with highly toxic organo-phosphate insecticides:*
Celery	Peaches		
Cherry tomatoes	Potatoes	*In addition to the Dirty Dozen, the EWG added two foods contaminated*	Hot peppers
Cucumbers	Snap peas		Kale/Collard greens
Grapes	Spinach		
	Strawberries		

2016 Clean Fifteen

Asparagus	Cauliflower	Mangoes	Sweet corn
Avocados	Eggplant	Onions	Sweet peas (frozen)
Cabbage	Grapefruit	Papayas	Sweet potatoes
Cantaloupe	Kiwis	Pineapples	

Measurement Conversions

VOLUME EQUIVALENTS (LIQUID)

US STANDARD	US STANDARD (OUNCES)	METRIC (APPROXIMATE)
2 tablespoons	1 fl. oz.	30 mL
¼ cup	2 fl. oz.	60 mL
½ cup	4 fl. oz.	120 mL
1 cup	8 fl. oz.	240 mL
1½ cups	12 fl. oz.	355 mL
2 cups or 1 pint	16 fl. oz.	475 mL
4 cups or 1 quart	32 fl. oz.	1 L
1 gallon	128 fl. oz.	4 L

OVEN TEMPERATURES

FAHRENHEIT (F)	CELSIUS (C) (APPROXIMATE)
250°F	120°C
300°F	150°C
325°F	165°C
350°F	180°C
375°F	190°C
400°F	200°C
425°F	220°C
450°F	230°C

VOLUME EQUIVALENTS (DRY)

US STANDARD	METRIC (APPROXIMATE)
⅛ teaspoon	0.5 mL
¼ teaspoon	1 mL
½ teaspoon	2 mL
¾ teaspoon	4 mL
1 teaspoon	5 mL
1 tablespoon	15 mL
¼ cup	59 mL
⅓ cup	79 mL
½ cup	118 mL
⅔ cup	156 mL
¾ cup	177 mL
1 cup	235 mL
2 cups or 1 pint	475 mL
3 cups	700 mL
4 cups or 1 quart	1 L
½ gallon	2 L
1 gallon	4 L

WEIGHT EQUIVALENTS

US STANDARD	METRIC (APPROXIMATE)
½ ounce	15 g
1 ounce	30 g
2 ounces	60 g
4 ounces	115 g
8 ounces	225 g
12 ounces	340 g
16 ounces or 1 pound	455 g

Resources

The following are my favorite brands of enameled cast iron cookware.

Le Creuset • LeCreuset.com

Staub • StaubUSA.com

Martha Stewart • Available at www.macys.com

Lodge • Lodgemfg.com

BOOKS

Davis, Hillary. *Le French Oven*. Layton, UT: Gibbs Smith, 2015.

Kramis, Sharon, and Julie Kramis Hearne. *The Dutch Oven Cookbook: Recipes for the Best Pot in Your Kitchen*. Seattle, WA: Sasquatch Books, 2014.

The Modern Dutch Oven Cookbook. Berkeley, CA: Rockridge Press, 2015.

REFERENCES

Grit. "Cast No Aspersions on Cast Iron Cookware." January 7, 2015. www.grit.com/community/history/cast-no-aspersions-on-cast-iron-cookware.aspx.

Ragsdale, John G. *Dutch Ovens Chronicled: Their Use in the United States*. Fayetteville, AR: University of Arkansas Press, 2016.

Recipe Index

Index

About the Author

ROBIN DONOVAN is a food writer, blogger, and recipe developer. She is the author of numerous cookbooks, including *Home Skillet*, *The Lazy Gourmet*, and the bestselling *Campfire Cuisine*. She lives in the San Francisco Bay Area with her husband and son. Find out more at www.RobinDonovan.com.

CPSIA information can be obtained
at www.ICGtesting.com
Printed in the USA
BVOW05s0634101216
470267BV00001B/1/P